ANTHROPOLOGY—
REALITY—
CINEMA

The Films of Jean Rouch

Edited by Mick Eaton

1979

Film Availability Services

General editor: Paul Willemen

British Film Institute, 127 Charing Cross Road, London WC2H OEA

Acknowledgments

I would like to thank the following people and organisations for their assistance and encouragement: Paul Willemen and Deirdre MacCloskey (BFI–FAS), the staff of the BFI's Information and Documentation Dept., David Meeker, Nigel Algar and Angela Martin of the BFI; Mme Françoise Foucault of the Musée de l'Homme in Paris; Mme Marielle Delorme of the S.E.R.D.D.A.V. in Ivry; Claudine Paquot of *Cahiers du Cinéma*; Judy Robinson for her help with German texts; Michael Brown and Felicity Oppé; John Higgins for his translations from French texts; Michel Marie; Tony Safford (*On Film*); Ivan Ward for his permission to re-work a section of our joint paper on ethnographic film given at the Communist University of London, summer 1978; Contemporary Films and Amanda Films; Les Editions Albatros for their kind permission to reprint Michel Marie's article; Secker & Warburg Ltd (Ms Gillian Vale) for their permission to use an extract from *Cinema: A Critical Dictionary*, edited by Richard Roud, to be published shortly; Mouton B. V. Uitgevery for permission to use an extract from Rouch's essay *The Camera and Man*; Tom Milne for his permission to make a few alterations to his translation of J.-A. Fieschi's article; Mr Fieschi himself; Lynda Myles for suggesting this project in the first place; and Peter Wollen for discussing Rouch's work and drawing attention to some of the theoretical and aesthetic issues involved.

Printed in Great Britain by
Spottiswoode Ballantyne Ltd., Colchester and London

Contents

CHRONICLE

Mick Eaton

The vast majority of Rouch's films are ethnographic shorts which have never been shown either publicly or privately in this country. Because of this it has been difficult to cross check all the titles, the dates and running times given here. The dates given for the films refer to the date of shooting, rather than the release date, although this is also given as often as possible. All unattributed quotes are taken from statements by or interviews with Jean Rouch.

The information on these shorts has for the most part been compiled from the following sources:

— *Images et Sons de la Recherche*, 1976 and 1978. Catalogues published by the Service d'Etude, de Réalisation et de Diffusion de Documents Audio-Visuels at the Centre National de la Recherche Scientifique (CNRS), Paris;

— *Image et Son*, no. 249, April 1971;

— Gilles Marsolais, *L'Aventure du Cinéma Direct*, Seghers, Paris, 1974;

— G. Roy Levin, *Documentary Explorations*, Doubleday, New York, 1971;

— *Filmkritik*, no. 253, 1978.

In cases where these sources provided conflicting information, the CNRS catalogues have been used as the sources most likely to be accurate.

Credit abbreviations are as follows: *d*—director; *p*—production; *ed*—editor; *sd*—sound; *ph*—camera.

1917	Jean Rouch born in Paris, the son of a naval officer who had accompanied Charcot on his second expedition to the South Pole. He studied at the Lycée Henri IV and trained as an engineer at l'Ecole des Ponts et Chaussées.
1936–1938	Margaret Mead and Gregory Bateson, financed by American universities, made a series of ethnographic films, entitled *Character Formation in Different Cultures: I—Bathing Babies; II—Childhood Rivalry in Bali and New Guinea; III—First Days in the Life of a New Guinea Baby.*
1941–1945	After graduation, during the occupation, he found work as a civil engineer in Niger. The following year he was expelled from there by the Petainist governor because of his gaullist sympathies and sent to Dakar. There is an apocryphal story from this time explaining the birth of his interest in anthropology: he was building a bridge when it started to thunder; the Songhays (people of the upper Niger) who were working on the construction, began to perform rituals which he observed in fascination. During this period he submitted written reports to Theodore Monod,

1

director of the Institut Français d'Afrique Noir (I.F.A.N.). After the liberation he returned to France and studied anthropology at the Musée de l'Homme.

1946   Rouch was taught by Marcel Griaule, who had worked extensively among the Dogon of Mali, studying, in particular, their cosmology; by Paul Rivet; and by Marcel Mauss, the founding father of modern French social anthropology, who had held a chair of sociology at the Collège de France since 1931. In 1946 Rouch and two friends prepared to make a trip down the Niger in a canoe. Griaule and Mauss had suggested to Rouch that on this trip he should try and record as much as possible by camera and sound recorder. The camera was regarded by them as the best tool for objectively recording technological practices. On two field-work trips in 1935 and 1938 Griaule had made two ethnographic shorts about the Dogon of the cliff of Bandiagara in Mali: *Au pays Dogon* and *Sur les masques noires* (which dealt with the role of the great masks in a funeral ceremony of the Dogon, a topic returned to by Rouch nearly thirty-five years later in *Funérailles du vieil Anai*). Griaule had made a distinction in relation to ethnographic filming between those films which were to be considered as 'works of art' and those which were 'notes of enquiry' a visual supplement of the anthropologist's notebook. (See, for example, his formulation of this argument in *Méthode de l'ethnographie*, 1957, a publication of the Faculty of Letters of Paris, pp. 85–89.) Rouch has written about Mauss's attitude to the use of the camera in anthropological enquiry in *Utilisation des techniques audio-visuelles pour la collecte et l'étude des sciences orales en Afrique* (Rapport UNESCO, October 1969, p. 8). He says: 'Mauss recommended to ethnographers the use of film to record certain modes of behaviour. He had not been able, because of his experience, to detect the specific nature of a filmic orientation; for him the camera was a visual memory which could record the totality of a phenomenon; by accumulating filmed archives one could eventually, for economic ends, make a short documentary film' (trans. M.R.E.).

It was under the influence of these sorts of ideas about the use of a camera in a field-work situation that Rouch and his two companions on the canoe trip, Jean Sauvy and Pierre Ponty, bought a second hand 16mm Bell and Howell in the flea market at Paris. Rouch was enthusiastic about this, having been, in his own words: 'one of the first adherents of the Cinémathèque Française'. At that time 16mm was an amateur format, although it had been used professionally by official photographers at the front lines during the war. Rouch learned how to load the camera flying over the Sahara. There is a mythological (in the Malinowskian sense of providing a charter for social action, in this instance Rouch's later film practice) story told of how early on in the expedition the tripod was lost over the side of the canoe, but Rouch soon realised how much more versatile it was to film without one. He was able to follow one particular action in detail, to move in close to it and move with it. This was at the expense of a certain instability of the image. It was during this trip, and on subsequent expeditions to Africa in the late forties and early fifties to study the migrations of the Sorkas from Niger to the coastal towns of West Africa and the fishermen of Niger, that Rouch's first ethnographic shorts were made.

2

1947   **Au pays des mages noirs** (In the land of the black magi)
p—Actualités Françaises. *d*—Jean Rouch, Jean Sauvy, Pierre Ponty.
16mm—b/w—15 mins.
Ritual of the Sorko fishermen hippopotamus hunters, filmed among the
Songhay in Niger.

1948   **Hombori**
The title is mentioned in Marsolais' book. No other information appears to
be available.

        Les magiciens de Wanzerbe (The Wanzerbe magicians)
p—CNRS and Secrétariat d'Etat à la Co-operation. *d*—Jean Rouch.
16mm—b/w—33 mins.
Principal rituals of the Songhay magicians in a Nigerian village. The
Wanzerbe market, children's games, Mossi the magician, dance of the
magicians, sacrifice made to the mountain 'protector' of the village.
According to Marsolais, this film was made in collaboration with R.
Rosfelder and Marcel Griaule.

        First ethnographic film conference at the Musée de l'Homme, Paris.

1949   **Circoncision** (Circumcision)
p—CNRS and Secrétariat d'Etat à la Co-operation. *d*—Jean Rouch.
16mm—colour—15 mins.
Prix du Reportage at the Festival of the Short Subject, Paris 1950.
Circumcision rites of 30 Songhay children from the village of Hombori in
Mali. The boys about to be circumcised are taken into the bush, prepared
and circumcised. After circumcision they are cared for and, in the evening,
they make their first appearance and sing the first song of the circumcised.

        Initiation à la danse des possedés (Initiation into the dance of the
possessed)
p—CNRS. *d*—Jean Rouch.
16mm—colour—25 mins.
First prize at the Festival of the Film Maudit, Biarritz.
A Songhay woman from the archipelago of Tillaberi (Niger) is initiated in
the ritual dances of possession. The musicians arrive. The first dance. The
dancing lesson: learning the main steps. Dance of departure of the initiated
and group dance.

1950– A series of five films made in collaboration with Roger Rosfelder, with
1952 whom Rouch was studying migration patterns.

        La chasse à l'hippopotame (The hippopotamus hunt)
d—Jean Rouch.
16mm—colour—36 mins.

        Yenendi: les hommes qui font la pluie (Yenendi: the men who make rain)
p—Institut Français d'Afrique Noire. *d*—Jean Rouch.
16mm—colour—35 mins.
Ritual ceremony of the 'Yenendi' among the Songhay of the village of
Simiri (Niger). The worshippers go in procession to the divinities' house to

3

celebrate the rain festival. The musicians make preparations and the dances of possession begin. The divinities express themselves through the voices of the dancers they have chosen. The priests sacrifice a ram before the end of the ceremony. The falling of the first rains.

Bataille sur le grand fleuve (Battle on the great river)
p—Institut Français d'Afrique Noire and Centre National du Cinéma.
d—Jean Rouch.
16mm—colour—25 mins.
The Sorko fishermen hunt the hippopotamuses of the Niger river with harpoons.

Les gens de mil (The man who grow millet)
d—Jean Rouch.
16mm—colour—31 mins.

Cimetière dans la falaise (Cemetery in the cliff)
p—CNRS and Secrétariat d'Etat à la Co-operation. *d*—Jean Rouch.
16mm—colour—20 mins.
Dogon funeral ritual on the death of a man in the village of Ireli (Mali). Sacrifice to the water divinity, funeral, burial, ritual condolence.

All of the short films made in this period focused on the classic topics of the ethnographic film as prescribed by Rouch's teachers: technology and ritual. However, during this period Rouch established working methods which he has adhered to ever since. The use of the hand-held camera has already been mentioned, but in addition to this Rouch developed the practice derived from Flaherty of returning to show the finished film to the people who had participated in its making. As he later put it, in an interview with Louis Marcorelles: 'It's impossible to make a film with the people concerned in your film if you stop contact with them when the film's finished.' [sic] However, for the film about the hippopotamus hunt Rouch had supplied a soundtrack in an attempt to convey some of the drama and tension of the hunt. He was criticised for this by the hunters as they said that it was necessary to keep absolutely silent when hunting. With very few exceptions the films of Rouch never have a soundtrack recorded at a different time from the filming. Others of these shorts had soundtracks composed of authentic African music recorded at approximately the same time as the filming using the Ichac and Scubitophone portable sound recorders.

1952   IVth International Congress of Anthropological and Ethnological Sciences at Vienna. During this Congress, the Comité International du Film Ethnographique et Sociologique was founded with Rouch appointed as Secretary-General (a role he has held ever since). Formed to 'establish links between the human sciences, and the cinematographic art, both from the point of view of the development of scientific research and for the expansion of the art of the motion picture', the CIFES (also referred to as CFE) has been involved with preparing lists and catalogues of ethnographic films for UNESCO, with producing films and distributing

4

films of interest to anthropologists. It is based at the Musée de l'Homme in Paris. Five of the ethnographic shorts were acquired by a commercial producer, blown up to 35mm, re-edited and eventually released commercially in 1955 as *Les fils de l'eau*. Rouch at first thought that an editor was superfluous (like a camera operator) but was pleased with the results when editing the films with Suzanne Baron, who had worked with Jacques Tati and later worked with Louis Malle. So another way of working was established for Rouch: he himself as cameraman/director, 'the first viewer', and an editor, someone who was not present at the shooting and not too familiar with the pro-filmic event as 'the second viewer'. The editor must 'tell me what he sees, and if he doesn't see something, then what I wanted to put in is not there, and if he sees something that I don't, then I have to take that into account' (Levin).

Les fils de l'eau (Sons of the water)
p—Films de la Pléiade. *d*—Jean Rouch. *ed.*—Suzanne Baron.
35mm—colour—75 mins.
Compilation film edited together from *Circoncision*; *Initiation à la danse des possedés*; *La chasse à l'hippopotame*; *Cimitière dans la falaise* and *Bataille sur le grand fleuve*. First shown in 1958.

1953 **Mammy Water**
p—Films de la Pléiade and CNRS. *d, ph, sd*—Jean Rouch.
16mm—colour—36 mins.
Re-edited in 1966, when a new soundtrack was added. Various aspects of the daily life of the Fanti of Shana (Ghana). Fishing techniques; funeral of a Fanti woman; ceremony honouring Mammy Water, the divinity of water, which opens the fishing season.

Alger-Le Cap
p—DOC. *d*—Serge de Poligny. *Consultant*—Jean Rouch.
16mm—b/w—102 mins.
Account of a car rally across the African continent.

1954 After eight years of war, France was defeated in Vietnam at the battle of Dien Bien Phu.
In Algeria, the Front de la Liberation Nationale (FLN) declares war on France. The Algerian War ended in 1962 with the defeat of both the French Government and the OAS, the guerilla army of the French settlers in Algiers.

1954– **Les maîtres fous** (Mad masters; The master madmen)
1955 *p*—Films de la Pléiade and CNRS. *d, ph* and *commentary*—Jean Rouch.
sd—Damouré Zika. *ed*—Suzanne Baron.
16/35mm—colour—36 mins.
Prix du Festival de Venise—Ethnographic Film Section. Released commercially in 1957 with Bergman's *Sawdust and Tinsel*.
This film, crucial to the development of Rouch's work and later ethnographic film practice, concerns the annual ceremonies of the Hauka cult which started in the late '20s in the Upper Niger region. Persecuted by the French colonial administration and denounced by orthodox Islam,

many of its practitioners moved to Ghana in the thirties, working as migrant labourers throughout the Gold Coast region. The Hauka are 'the new Gods', spirits of power and of the winds. During the ceremonies the initiates become possessed by these powerful spirits which take (the form of figures of authority in the Western colonial administration (the Governor-General, the Admiral, etc.). In a state of trance the possessed take on these roles and act like the white figures of authority. The members of the cult had also evolved a peculiar kind of pidgin, used in the ceremonies and unique to them. Expelled from Ghana following independence the Hauka returned to their original lands and the cult gradually died out as the models of colonial power and authority disappeared. The film is a record of a Hauka ceremony during which the participants become possessed, a dog is ritually sacrificed and eaten. The film also includes footage of the Western figures whose power the Hauka spirits personify. The thesis of the film advanced by Rouch in the commentary is that the ritual plays a therapeutic role in the lives of the marginalised and oppressed people, allowing them to accommodate to the psychological disjunctions caused by colonialism. At the end of the film we are shown the Hauka priests back at work on the roads or in the markets of Accra. The commentary is an attempt to provide an anthropological explanation/rationale for the 'bizarre' or 'exotic' nature of much of the footage, shifting the terms of emphasis so that it is the colonial admini-stration which emerges as bizarre and irrational.

Rouch was asked to make the film after he and his wife, Jane, had given a lecture at the British Council in Accra. In the audience there were several Hauka priests and initiates, many of whom originally came from the area of Upper Niger where the shorts shown by Rouch at that lecture had been filmed. He was approached by them and asked to make a film of their annual ceremony. The priests wanted a film not only as a record of the ceremony but also so that it could be used in the ritual itself. Whilst in Accra, Rouch attended many of the smaller Hauka ceremonies and was cabled by the priests on 15 August, 1954, in Togo, where he was travelling, to return as the big ceremony was about to be held.

The film was shot on a hand-cranked 16mm Bell and Howell camera which allowed for 25 sec. shots, but it was edited in the camera as much as possible and the eventual shooting ratio was only about 8–10. The sound was recorded by Damouré Zika, one of the first Africans Rouch had got to know well on his first trip during the war, using a Scubitophone which is a portable though heavy tape-recorder with a clockwork motor that had to be wound up between takes.

When shown in Paris, the film was widely criticised. Black students in the audience accused Rouch of reinforcing stereotypes of 'savagery', and the film was banned throughout Britain's African colonies because of its 'inflammatory' content. Jean Genet's play *The Blacks*—in which colonised people act out the roles of the colonisers—was heavily influenced by it and Peter Brook used it as a model for his actors during the rehearsals of *Marat/Sade*. Rouch has always defended the film, not only on the basis of its ethnographic veracity and his commitment to the use of film in 'describing' a ceremony (where there are many simultaneous events which are impossible to convey adequately through the medium of print) but also, and more significantly, in relation to his later film practice, because the

6

content of the film is concerned specifically with the intermingling of cultures and the effects—particularly the psychological effects—of colonialism. Unlike the vast majority of ethnographic films, including Rouch's early shorts, *Les maîtres fous* does not construct African culture as somehow occupying a sphere discrete in itself and unaffected by Western contact.

During this period Rouch was still working on his ethnographic study of migration patterns in West Africa, eventually published as *Migrations au Ghana (Gold Coast)—Enquête 1953–55* in the Journal de la Societé des Africanistes, no. 26, pp. 33–196 (1956). In 1954, he also started filming *Jaguar*, which was not completed and released until 1967. In order to deal with a 'big event' such as the seasonal migrations of the Songhay from Niger to Ghana and the Ivory Coast, it was necessary to move into fiction, using 'benevolent actors' (Damouré Zika, Lam Ibrahim Dia, Illo Gaoudel, all friends of Rouch and themselves migrants). Rouch has said that fiction allowed him to tell a story which emphasised the important aspects, whereas with an ethnographic documentary 'one is obliged to show almost everything'. The finished film deals with changes in these patterns of migration over time in relation to the changing political situation.

1955   In the summer of 1955 there was a short season of ethnographic films at the Musée de l'Homme. In addition to films by Flaherty, Bunuel and Eisenstein, the following films were shown:
Circoncision, Mammy Water, Les maîtres fous (Rouch), *Stone-Age People* (Mountford-Villeminot), *Days Without End* (Wilkinson), *The Muruts of North Borneo* (Ivan Polunin), *Fête chez les Hamba, Ruanda* (Zangrie), *Bororo, Samba* (Henry Brandt), *Ballet Kandyan* (Morilliere), *Pasqua in Sicilia* (Pandolfi), *Les hommes d'Amok* (Drilhon), *Precolumbian Art* (Fulchignoni), *Carnaval de Binche* (Cleinge and Boe), *Iawa* (Flornoy), *Fiestas* (Fain), *Israel* (Grjebene), *Les fils de l'éléphant* (Philipe-Paques).
To accompany this series of screenings Rouch wrote an article in *Positif* 14/15, 1955 entitled *A Propos de Films Ethnographiques*, in which he attempted to define the 'mysterious quality' of ethnographic films and the differences between filming people and writing about them.

1957   On 6 March, Ghana, formely the Gold Coast, becomes the first African colony to gain independence.

Baby Ghana (Independence festivities in Ghana)
p—CNRS. d—Jean Rouch.

Moi, un noir (Me, a black man)
p—Films de la Pleïade—Pierre Braunberger, Roger Fleytoux and CNRS. d, ph—Jean Rouch. *Commentary*—Oumarou Ganda. *Consultant*—Lam Ibrahim Dia. sd—Andre Lubin. ed—Marie-Joseph Yoyotte, Catherine Dourgnant.
Cast: Oumarou Ganda (Edward G. Robinson), Touré Mohammed (Eddie Constantine-Lemmy Caution), Alassane Maiga (Tarzan), Mlle. Gambi (Dorothy Lamour) (all non-professional actors).
35/16mm—colour—80 mins.
Obtained the Prix Delluc in 1959.

Moi, un noir was Rouch's first feature length film. Shot in Treichville, a slum/suburb of Abidjan in the Ivory Coast, the film continues many of the themes of earlier work (especially *Jaguar* and *Les maîtres fous*): immigration to the coastal towns, contact of colonisers and colonised, the effects of colonialism and proletarianisation. An attempt to 'mix fiction with reality', it follows the daily routine of three young men from Niger working as casual labourers in Abidjan. The characters were asked to play out their lives in front of the camera (some of the background of this is described in Oumarou Ganda's piece reprinted below). In a sense, the characters are seen as already living out a 'fictional reality' in Treichville, far from their homes and traditional lives in Niger. They all adopt the pseudonyms of famous movie stars, which is seen as a way of coping with their lives in Abidjan (a classic sociological explanation) making the concerns of this film, if not its form, very close to those of *Les maîtres fous*. Rouch describes them as 'trying to reconstitute every saturday and sunday a sort of mythological Eldorado, based on boxing, the cinema, love and money.' The film was shot silent and the commentary spoken by Oumarou Ganda whilst the rushes were being projected. In relation to the film Rouch has said: 'Fiction is the only way to penetrate reality—the means of sociology remain exterior ones. In *Moi, un noir* I wanted to show an African city—Treichville. I could have made a documentary full of figures and observations. That would have been deathly boring. So I told a story with characters, their adventures and their dreams. And I didn't hesitate to introduce the dimensions of the imaginary, of the unreal—when a character dreams he's boxing, he boxes ... the whole problem is to maintain a certain sincerity towards the spectator, never to mask the fact that this is a film ... once this sincerity is achieved, when nobody is deceiving anybody, what interests me is the introduction of an imaginary, of the unreal. I can then use the film to tell what cannot be told otherwise.' (*Télérama*, no. 872. Trans. M.R.E.)

The film was censored in the Ivory Coast by the government. Rouch attributes this to the fact that it dealt with 'a person in the street, a tramp rather than a lawyer or a doctor—a bourgeois.' The French colonial administration also tried to ban it throughout France's African colonies because in one scene the black protagonist fights with a white merchant seaman.

Godard admitted to the film as an influence on his work, calling it 'the best French film since the liberation.' After making the film Oumarou Ganda was trained by French film maker acquaintances of Rouch in Niamey and is now a film maker in Niger.

Extracts from the scenario of this film were published in *Cahiers du Cinéma*, no. 90, 1958.

The following text by Oumarou Ganda, the 'star' of *Moi, un noir*, was published, along with a similar text by Touré Mohammed (who played 'Eddie Constantine') as part of an article by Claude Jutra, *En Courant Derrière Rouch* in *Cahiers du Cinéma*, no. 113, November 1960. The text was given to Jutra by Jane Rouch. The date referred to by Ganda as the time of shooting is incorrect. Jutra was in Abidjan in April 1959, while *Moi, un noir* was made two years earlier.

EDWARD ROBINSON

My Life and Adventures in Treichville

Oumarou Ganda

It was on 20 April, 1959 (sic) that the boss, Jean Rouch, suggested making a film with me. The cinema interests me, yes, I've always wanted to be a great cinema actor.

For a long time, even before Jean Rouch suggested it to me, I wanted to be an actor, because I believe in the cinema very much. It was after this that I asked the boss how the cineaste who made 'Superman' had managed to make him fly. Was it because he had wings?

To cut a long story short, let's get down to facts.

I was working as an unskilled labourer every day at the customs, carrying sacks of coffee, cocoa, wheat flour, etc. (making 225 francs a day). To tell the truth I was doing this work just to survive, so as not to die of hunger or to steal.

Moreover, being an unskilled labourer shouldn't have been my job: I studied for seven years at the primary school at Niamey, I did four years of military service, two years and one month at war, of which six months was on the front line, in the sector of Sontay, at Tonkin, Indo-China. I had been to war before I was twenty years old. Really its beneath me to be an unskilled labourer.

The first day of shooting was a saturday. I found myself in front of a boutique, 'Treichville Elegance'. It was a saturday night, like any other saturday night in Treichville. For me there was nothing different. The boss, Rouch, asked me to go for my saturday night walk, without doing anything different from normal.

Without understanding anything, I started to walk, followed by M. Jean Rouch and lots of curious people. Moreover, I didn't even have the right to try and find out what was going on; I'd come to the Ivory Coast to look for money and I was sure this white man wasn't going to tire me out without giving me a sou; so I had to walk.

We'd just started shooting when up came Alassane Maiga ('Tarzan' in the film) and Petit Touré ('Eddie Constantine'), who' been looking for me. I was in front of 'Treichville-Elegance' choosing beautiful shirts and shoes, without a penny in my pocket.

After we'd shot a little in front of the shop, the invitation was made to go to the dancing bar 'Esperance'. Normally it's Maiga and Touré who would have done it, but that night it was M. Rouch who made the suggestion.

We shot a little in the 'Esperance' and danced as well. I was a little tired and asked for a break to go back home. My holiday was over, as it's only on saturday night that I get any time off. So saturday night finished like that.

9

During the week M. Rouch would not leave me for a moment. The morning after the saturday night, a gentleman was asking for me: it's a European, it's M. Rouch. And he followed me all day with his camera in his hand. I was treated like an idiot because I was making a film, but it wasn't a normal film, because I was telling the story of my private life. And I reply: 'This is not my country and here I am my own master. I agree, I'm coming.'

People who are more informed than me, to whom I talked, asked me: 'How much has he given you in advance? Not even a hundred thousand francs!' And I reply: 'No, how could I have made a hundred thousand francs for a day's work when I'm still doing my usual work as a daily porter at the port of Abidjan for 225 francs a day.'

The same people led me to understand that films are very expensive. I began to believe them. One day, moreover, I read in the newspaper *Abidjan Matin* that Eddie Constantine earns 800 million francs for a single film. It's true then. I took the paper to my boss Rouch who told me: 'It's not possible, you can't have 800 million like Eddie, besides, you're not an actor'. That's what he told me.

And I reply: 'Why not? How come Eddie Constantine earns 800 million francs for a film and I don't? Is it just my luck or what? Is it because I'm black?'

The film was silent.

I was asked to do the commentary. I didn't know what a commentary was, and still I felt rebellious: those guys must be right, it's a trick. The boss knew he could get me where he wanted me by offering me a beer, my cure for the blues, and some money.

I saw the film: it's perfect. The film was a bloody nuisance to me, for while it was being made I didn't get any rest. When I came from work at midday I was told to wait without resting: he had to film me coming out of work. In the morning, before going out to work, M. Rouch comes with me, because he wants to film me going to the port. If I want to go to Port-Bouet the boss wants to come with me.

There were certain places where I didn't want him to go, but as I had sworn to be frank and as I had said that I would, nothing could stop me from going there with him in spite of the embarrassment that his presence caused me. Anyway, as far as the shooting goes, that's it. Let us move on to the present.

Today things aren't going too badly. For a start *Treichville* has changed its name [*Moi, un noir*]. The papers, the press, the letters written to Gambi-Dorothy Lamour and many other things have still made me believe in, if not millions, to tell the truth, but in a lot of money.

I think that those who have seen my image, who have heard my commentary, who don't want to do me any harm or treat me like an idiot, say to me: 'S'il vous plaît, Monsieur Oumarou Ganda!' In any case that's what I think.

You ought to know that I no longer dream of being a world champion boxer. A cinema actor, well perhaps I will never be one, it's a big never, but it's my dream which has remained engraved in my mind. But if ever the opportunity presents itself to me that I, Oumarou Ganda, will make another film, then I swear that I will beat all the professional actors, not only the French, but those from the whole of the international film world of today.

Besides, why shouldn't I be an actor? Aren't I just as much of a Frenchman as the rest because we have the same fatherland? I have risked my life twenty-four hours a day on the field of battle. In my twenty years I have found myself on the battlefield in Indo-China, at Tonkin. Why then shouldn't I become an actor, my biggest dream?

Anyway, I await the future, for it will make me an actor. By the way, I forgot to tell you about my fight with that dirty rotten Italian, a sailor on a ship whose name I don't know, over the charming Dorothy Lamour, the Nigerian girl, whom I know from my country, who has taken advantage of my money ever since I came from Indo-China.

Because, take note, I was not born to be a labourer, far from it. Moreover, in my country I wouldn't be able to do it. I consider work like that unworthy of me. My friends who were in the film with me, Alassane Maiga, a taxi-driver in Treichville, and Petit Touré, the stevedore and salesman of fabrics, all are still in Treichville today, like me.

Translated by Mick Eaton.

1958   Rouch was invited to attend the fifth Flaherty Seminar, organised by Frances Flaherty, Hugh Grey and Philip Chamberlain at the University of California at Santa Barbara. Here he gave a lecture, showed several films (*Les fils de l'eau, Les maîtres fous* and *Moi, un noir*) and met other film makers who were involved in making ethnographic shorts, many of them state sponsored. Other films shown include: *Together* by Lorenza Mazzetti and Denis Horne, financed by the British Film Institute; *Santero* (The Saintmaker) and *El Puente* (The Bridge) by Amilcar Tirado and financed by the Community Education division of Puerto Rico; *The Hunters* by John Marshall and Robert Gardner, financed by the BFI, and, crucially, *Les Raquetters* (The Snowshoers) by Michel Brault and G. Groulx, financed by the Office National du Film (ONF), Quebec. Rouch talked to the Canadians about their experiments with hand-held cameras and wide angle lenses. Two years later he was to invite Brault over to France to be the camera operator for *Chronique d'un été*.

Moro Naba
p—CNRS and the Institut Français d'Afrique Noire. d—Jean Rouch. ed—Jean Ravel. *Consultant*—Prof. Dim Zahan.
16mm—colour—28 mins.
Funeral ceremony of the Moro Naba, traditional leader of the Mossi of Ouagadougou region (Upper Volta). Election ceremonies for his successor. Preparing the feast for the end of mourning. Ceremony in the palace, the people of Ouagadougou, the warriors in traditional dress. Presentation of new leader.

La royale goumbé
p—CNRS/CFE. d—Jean Rouch.

Film of a goumbé, a society formed by migrants in the coastal towns of West Africa.

Sakpata
p—CNRS/CFE. d—Jean Rouch with Gilbert Rouget.
16mm—colour—25 mins.
Leaving ritual of four novices from a monastery at Sakpata in Dahomey.

1959 **La pyramide humaine** (The human pyramid)
p—Films de la Pléiade. d, ph—Jean Rouch. sd—Michel Fano.
Cast (non-professional actors): Nadine, Denise, Alain, Jean-Claude and the students of the Lycée d'Abidjan.
35/16mm—colour—80 mins.
Filmed 1959–60, released April 1961.
The film arose again from Rouch's interest in the clash of cultures in the towns of West Africa. His idea was to make a film about the relationships between black and white students in the leaving class of the Lycée d'Abidjan (the title of the film is from a poem by Paul Eluard about the dreams and loves of college students). In fact, the two racial groups in the school had very little to do with each other. This led Rouch to work out a fictional scenario. The two groups of students agreed to work together whilst the film was being made and Rouch 'invented' the plot: the arrival of Nadine, a new girl who was white and who wanted to get to know the black students. The students were instructed to play roles which arose from their own behaviour, leading to a drama described as 'fictive, but plausible' (Marsolais) similar to the therapeutic practice of socio- or psycho-drama.

Rouch had been impressed with the discussion scenes in *We are the Lambeth Boys* and included similar scenes here (the students discussing South Africa, life in Abidjan, etc.). Also in this film there is a sequence in which the students and Rouch watch the rushes of the film and decide where to go from there—a technique he developed in *Chronique d'un été*. In this film, we see for the first time in Rouch's work an attempt at cine-provocation: the idea that the camera acts as a catalyst, not a neutral recording device, and that the presence of the camera is responsible for creating the responses of the people being filmed. 'The camera was not an obstacle to expression, rather it was an indispensable witness which made that expression possible.' (Rouch quoted in *Cahiers du Cinéma*, no. 112, 1960.)

At the time of shooting *La pyramide humaine* there was no light weight sync-sound system available. For some of the discussion scenes Rouch used a blimped Cameflex 16 (weighing approx. 50 kgs) which was placed an equal distance from each of the principal actors who were told to wait until the camera was pointing at them before replying to a question. However, the bulk of the soundtrack was recorded when the rushes were complete. Rouch's intention had been to construct a soundtrack in a similar way to that of *Moi, un noir*, but during the nine months of shooting relationships between the students had developed and it was impossible to recapture the apparent spontaneity of the events on the soundtrack. When Rouch asked them to improvise a commentary, nothing happened, 'because their commentary was a memory of their holidays, the memory of

12

an exciting adventure they had been through, but it wasn't their true adventure.' Rouch even went to the extent of reconstructing some of the scenes, but as the students had changed so much during the course of the filming, the film emerges as a documentary 'about' being in a film by Rouch. (As Richard Leacock has said, 'It seems to me that although his films are so interesting, the most important thing that has ever happened to the people he chooses to film is the fact that he has filmed them.' *Cahiers du Cinéma*, no. 140, February 1963.) Because of these factors, judgements of the film tend to attribute its 'lack of success', however inadequately defined, to purely technical hitches. (For instance Marsolais says that *La pyramide humaine* suffers from 'deficiencies of a purely technical order.') But Rouch has said of the film: 'For me, the essential result remains to have been able to show how a community becomes aware of segregation and the absurdities it engenders.' (*Le Monde*, 22 December, 1960.) It is clear from this statement that Rouch sees his major responsibility as being towards his 'actors', rather than towards any possible audience. This tends to validate Leacock's opinion and also points towards one of the major differences between the film practice of Rouch and that of the Leacock–Pennebaker–Maysles school in the States. Two contradictory stories circulate in relation to this aspect of Rouch's work. The first comes from an interview Rouch gave on the BBC with Louis Marcorelles (November 1960) where he said that being in the film not only led to friendships and understanding between the students of different races, but that it also improved their exam results. However, in his article on Rouch in *Film Comment*, James Blue maintains that because of their involvement in the film several of the students flunked their exams. As in the films of Rouch the truth of a statement seems to be a function of the particular discourse in which it is placed, rather than something which can be unproblematically arrived at. Both Nadine and Landry, who appear in the film, have been used by Rouch time and again, becoming part of his 'stock company'. Once again, the film was censored throughout Africa.

The scenario of *La pyramide humaine* was published in *Cahiers du Cinéma*, no. 112, 1960.

Release of *A bout de souffle*, by Jean-Luc Godard.

1960   Niger and Mali achieve independence.

Chronique d'un été (Chronicle of a summer)
p—Argos Films. *d*—Jean Rouch and Edgar Morin. *ph*—Roger Morilliere, Raoul Coutard, Jean-Jacques Tarbes, Michel Brault. *ed.*—Jean Ravel, Nena Baratier, Françoise Colin.
Cast (non-professional actors): Marceline, Mary-Lou, Angelo, Jean-Pierre; Workers: Jacques and Jean; Students: Regis, Celine, Jean-Marie, Nadine, Landry, Raymond; Employers: Jacques and Simone; Artists: Henri, Madi, Catherine; Model: Sophie.
16mm—b/w—90 mins.
Filmed: summer of 1960; released: October 1961.
Prizes at Manheim, Cannes and Venice festivals.
Rouch was approached by the sociologist Edgar Morin to make a film about Paris. Morin had long been interested in the cinema (he wrote *Le Cinéma, ou l'homme imaginaire* and *Les Stars*) and had praised Rouch's

work in an article *Pour un nouveau cinéma-vérité* in *France Observateur*, no. 506, 14 January, 1960. Morin had been a member of the resistance during the war and was expelled from the Communist Party in 1951 for his opposition to Stalinism. At this time he was also editor of the review *Arguments*. Morin's idea was to make a 'sociological fresco' (Rouch: '*je ne suis pas fresqueur.*') about Paris in the summer of 1960, when it was thought that the Algerian war was going to end. Rouch was interested but admitted to knowing very little about what was happening in Paris at that time. Although he had so often talked of the importance of being well acquainted with the people he was filming, most of the people involved in *Chronique* were Morin's friends, many of them members of a leftist group, *Socialisme ou Barbarie*, who had left the French Communist Party after the events in Hungary. Rouch has since talked of the difficulties of working with a collaborator: 'Working with Morin was exciting during the planning, but annoying during the shooting.' Rouch and Morin were given an entirely free hand by the producer and worked with the participants over several months without interference. The film was subtitled '*une experience de cinéma-vérité*' (apparently in hommage to Dziga Vertov, but this point will be examined more closely elsewhere in the monograph) and whilst it was in no sense a 'psycho-drama' like *La pyramide humaine*, the founding ideas were very similar: the camera was to act as a 'catalyst', and 'accelerator' making people reveal themselves. However, it is worth mentioning that Rouch found the French much more camera shy than the Africans he had been filming for so many years.

In many respects the importance of his film lies in the way it was made and the technological innovations that accompanied it. Shooting started with the standard Arriflex, which, although reasonably light at 10 kgs, was noisy. Rouch's French cameraman was not prepared to walk with it in the street sequences, so Rouch contacted Brault, whom he had met at the Flaherty seminar (see above), and who had experimented with a hand-held blimped Arriflex. Some of the street-interview scenes at the beginning of the film and the sequence in the Renault factory were shot by Raoul Coutard from a long distance, without the knowledge of the people being filmed, using the hand-held Arriflex. At the same time Rouch was in contact with André Coutant, who worked at the Eclair factory, and who had been instrumental in the development of the Cameflex which Rouch had been using for some of the interview sequences. Coutant introduced him to a new camera which was being developed for use in a space satellite for purposes of military surveillance. This camera was light (6 kgs), dependable, and virtually silent, but it had only a magazine of 3 minutes worth of film. Coutant worked on the camera as the film progressed in an attempt to extend the capacity of the magazine. Every night Rouch would return the camera to Coutant at the Eclair factory and discuss any problems that had arisen. Eclair had a contract with the producers of the film which absolved them from all responsibility regarding malfunctions, such as scratches of the film stock as it passed through the mechanism.

This camera was the prototype of the KMT Coutant-Mathot Eclair, the first light, silent portable 16mm camera with sync-sound. It was used in a famous scene in *Chronique* where Marceline walks through Les Halles with a Nagra tape recorder in her handbag, reminiscing to herself about her wartime experiences of deportation, whilst the camera (placed on the back seat of a 2 CV) moves away from her. The development of the camera freed the crew to get out into the streets and move about holding the camera, and the new possibility of sync-sound had its effect on the film, making it much more a film 'about' people talking, rather than them acting out their lives in front of the camera.

The K.M.T. was subsequently used by Mario Ruspoli (*Les inconnus de la terre*) and Chris Marker (*Le joli mai*) and had a profound influence on all aspects of film making, including television documentary practice and the sync-sound work of Godard in 35mm. The film again raises the questions of what happens to 'ordinary people' after Rouch has given them the possibility of being, for a few short months, movie stars. Marceline (Loridan) married Joris Ivens and has worked throughout the world with him; Jean-Pierre (Sergent) made movies in Algeria and Colombia: Regis (Debray) went to Cuba to make a film about Che Guevara. He subsequently went to Colombia, where he was arrested and imprisoned for revolutionary activity; he is the author of *'Revolution in the Revolution'* and other books about revolution. Mary-Lou became a stills photographer who worked with Bertolucci and Godard. There were more problems with Angelo, the worker in the Renault plant. He was fired because of his involvement in the film and got work at the Billancourt Studios where he was fired for his political activity. Morin pulled strings to get him a job at the publishing firm, Editions du Seuil, but when he tried to organise a union there too, there was a certain amount of embarrassment caused, so 'we gave him money to buy a small workshop in Levallois where he worked as a mechanic'.

There were 21 hrs of rushes from which the finished film was edited. The immense difficulty of cutting led Rouch to consider making another film in Paris where the action would take place in a single day. Although the film was released around the world, and was well received critically, it was not a success commercially.

The scenario of *Chronique*, together with articles by Rouch and Morin and interviews with the participants, was published in *Interspectacles*, *Domaine Cinéma 1*, Cahiers trimestrials, Winter 61–62, Paris.

La punition (Punishment)
p—Films de la Pléiade. d—Jean Rouch. ph—Michel Brault, Roger Morilliere, Georges Dufault. *Music*—Johann Christian Bach. ed—Anne Tresgot.
Cast (non-professional actors): Nadine Ballot (Nadine), Jean-Marie Simon (the engineer), Jean-Claude Darnal (the student), Landry (the black man from Abidjan).
16mm—b/w—58 mins.
Shown on French television (O.R.T.F.) on 10 March 1962.
Shot in October 1960.
This film was the result of the attempt to impose a rigid time structure on the shooting in order to cut down on the amount of film to be edited. It was meant to be shot in one day, but as it turned out, it took a whole weekend. The film was also a deliberate attempt to apply the 'techniques' of cinema vérité, developed in *Chronique* (hand-held camera, long takes, outside locations, improvised dialogue, etc.) to a fictional story. The 'plot' of the film is very simple, based on what Rouch describes as a 'surrealist pre-

occupation', the chance meeting, and with a fictional form apparently developed from *commedia dell'arte*. Nadine is thrown out of school for the day, for arriving late. Unable to return home she wanders through Paris where she meets three men: a student, an engineer and a black African 'representing love, money and adventure' respectively. The camera work by Brault consisted of ten minute takes (using the K.M.T.). Nadine had a Nagra hidden in her handbag and all the characters were supplied with portable microphones.

However, they had obtained six hours of rushes from the weekend's work, all composed of ten minute takes and all extremely hard to edit because of Brault's elaborate movements during shooting. When the editing was completed the emphasis of the characters had changed dramatically: 'In the rushes the student was wonderful and the engineer was ridiculous', after editing, these adjectives could be reversed.

The film was premiered at the UNESCO Club in Paris, where it was heavily criticised by Roberto Rossellini, who accused Rouch of laziness. Some of the background to this is discussed in a long interview with Rouch conducted by Louis Marcorelles and Eric Rohmer in *Cahiers du Cinéma*, no. 144, June 1963.

Publication of *Essai sur la Religion Songhay* [Essay on Songhay Religion] by Rouch, Presses Universitaires de France, Paris.

Release of *Primary* (Richard Leacock) and *Yanki No* (Leacock, Maysles, Pennebaker).

1961 Les ballets de Niger
Film of the ballet company of Niger, shot in Paris by Rouch.

Niger, jeune republique
p—ONF (Quebec). *d*—Claude Jutra. *Adviser*—Jean Rouch.
Assistants—Roger Morilliere and Susanne Vianes.
16mm—b/w—58 mins.
Made to commemorate the first anniversary of the independence of Niger. Versions in the Zerma and Hausa languages were made for exhibition in Niger. For more information regarding Jutra and Morilliere's adventures with Rouch in Africa, see *En courant derrière Rouch*, by Jutra in *Cahiers du Cinéma*, nos. 113, 115 and 116, November 1960, January and February 1961.

Script, a Belgian magazine, publishes an interview with Rouch.

1962 Abidjan—port de pêche (Abidjan—fishing port)
p—CFE/CNRS. *d*—Jean Rouch.
16mm—colour—25 mins.
Film about the differences between traditional and industrial fishing in the Gulf of Guinea.

Fêtes de l'indépendence de Niger (Independence festivities in Niger)
p—CNRS/CFE and IFAN (Niger). *d*—Jean Rouch. (Filmed in December 1961).
16mm—colour—27 min.

Le palmier à l'huile (Palm oil)
p—CNRS/CFE and IFAN. *d*—Jean Rouch.
16mm—colour—18 mins.
Film of agricultural research on the cultivation of palm oil in the Ivory Coast. This film and *Le cocotier* are, in effect, 'educational films' and Rouch has subsequently mentioned how bored he was making them.

Le cocotier (The coconut palm tree)
p—CFE/CNRS. *d*—Jean Rouch.
16mm—colour—17 mins.

Les pêcheurs de Niger (The fishermen of the Niger)
p—CNRS/CFE. *d*—Jean Rouch.

Urbanisme Africain (African Urbanism)
d—Jean Rouch.

Le mil (Millet)
p—CFE/CNRS. *d*—Jean Rouch. *Assistants*—Roger Rosfelder, Louis Civatte and Moustapha Alassane.
16mm—colour—20 mins.
Film dealing with the agricultural cycle of millet cultivation in the savannah region of Niger and the accompanying ritual.

Rose et Landry
p—ONF (Quebec). *d*—Jean Rouch. *ph*—Georges Dufault. *sd*—Marcel Carriere. *ed*—Jacques Godebout.
16mm—b/w—28 mins.
Commissioned by the National Film Board of Canada as part of a series entitled *Ceux qui parlent français*. Shot in Abidjan, the film features Landry returning to his home after a period as a student in Paris. Four hours of rushes were obtained, concentrating on Landry's position as an African caught between two cultures. The editing was apparently carried out in Canada without Rouch's supervision, and includes several techniques alien to Rouch's own practice, such as the over-dubbing of sound onto an image track recorded elsewhere, and cross cutting between the scenes in which Landry and Rose talk of their aspirations and footage of traditional West African village life.

Publication of '*Le Cinéma et les Sciences Sociales*' (UNESCO) by Luc de Heusch, with a preface by Morin.

Article on Rouch in *Image et Son*, no. 119.

First appearance in England of *Movie* magazine, introducing an anglicised version of *auteur* criticism into the U.K. through articles concentrating largely on Hollywood cinema and the French New Wave. There is an article on *Chronique* in issue no. 2, September 1962.

1963   **Monsieur Albert, Prophète**
p—Argos Films (Paris) and CNRS. *d*, *ph* and *commentary*—Jean Rouch. *ed*—Jean Ravel.
35/16mm—colour—27 mins.
Ethnographic short about the Harris sect in Bregbo, Ivory Coast, and their High Priest, Albert Atcho.

January: interview with Rouch by Raymond Bellour and Maurice Frydland, entitled *Aux sources du cinéma-vérité avec Jean Rouch* in *Cinéma 63*, no. 72.

March: three day study conference on Cinéma Vérité at Lyon, organised by Radio Television Française. Reported in special issue of *Movie*, no. 8, April 1963, which includes an interview with Rouch.

Long interview with Rouch by Eric Rohmer and Louis Marcorelles, together with analyses of some films, in *Cahiers du Cinéma*, no. 144, June 1963.

Publication of *Le Cinéma et la Vérité*, edited by Raymond Bellour as a special issue of *Artsept*. Pp. 55–69 are on Rouch. The article by L. Goldmann published in this monograph first appeared in that issue of *Artsept*.

1964   **Les veuves de quinze ans** (The fifteen year old widows)

A section of the Italian–Canadian–Japanese–French co-production *La fleur de l'age—Les adolescents*. Other sections were directed by Hiroshi Teshigahara, Michel Brault and Gian Vittorio Baldi.

p—Films de la Pleïade. *d*—Jean Rouch. *ph*—Jacques Lang. *ed*—Claudine Bouché. *sd*—Michel Fano.

Cast (non-professional actors): Véronique Duval, Marie-France de Chabenix, Nadine Ballot, Marc Kalinoski, Michel Aracheguesne, Eliane Bonneau, Olivier Perrin, Leporrier, Gilles Queant, Didier Leon, Maurice Pialla.

16mm—colour—25 mins.

Alternative title: *Marie-France et Véronique.*

Another experiment around the problems of psycho-drama: the story of two girls 'one who becomes delinquent, the other who does not'. The dialogue was written in advance in collaboration with the two girls, but at the time of shooting their roles were exchanged. Rouch: 'I have reversed the roles because I have learned by experience that being in a film can have a certain effect on a non-professional performer. It's quite troubling to put people in a film, forcing them to play their own role—either because they feel guilty afterwards or because they become exhibitionists'.

The film was censored. Rouch had to cut out all 'obscene words' the girls used and, interestingly, the opinions they expressed about their families. Rouch: 'Those poor girls were stilted, devoured by anxiety. I really have a horrible memory of it, it was like forced labour, military service. *Gare du Nord* was a reaction against *Veuves*'.

Gare du Nord

A section of the feature length film *Paris vu par*. Other sections were directed by Jean-Daniel Pollet, Jean Douchet, Eric Rohmer, Claude Chabrol and Jean-Luc Godard.

p—Les Films du Losange. *d*—Jean Rouch. *ph*—Etienne Becker. *ed*—Jacqueline Raynal.

Cast: Nadine Ballot (*Odile*), Barbet Schroeder (*Jean-Pierre*), Gilles Queant (*the desperate man*).

16mm—colour—16 mins. Released in October 1965.

An attempt to deal more directly with fiction while simultaneously endeavouring to achieve an exact correspondence between film time and real time. With the exception of establishing and closing shots the film is composed of two ten minute takes with the change-over disguised as the camera operator changed the magazine in the darkness at the bottom of an elevator, so that there appears to be no interruption in movement. The camera movements had been worked out meticulously in advance with the camera operator and the actors, but even so the first part had to be shot seven times and the second shot three times before it worked correctly. The 'story', briefly, concerns a young woman who argues with her husband because their life is dull, and walks out on him. She meets a stranger who invites her to run away with him, but she refuses and he commits suicide. Rouch: 'We live through everything leading up to the suicide; in a sense, we too become involved and, in a way, responsible for the suicide.'

Interview published in *Image et Son*, no. 173.

1964– 1965   **L'Afrique et la recherche scientifique** (Africa and scientific research)
p—CNRS for UNESCO. *d*—Jean Rouch.
16mm—colour—31 mins.

Alpha noir (Black Alpha)
p—CNRS/CFE. *d*—Jean Rouch.

Tambours de pierre (Drums of stone)
p—CNRS/CFE. *d*—Jean Rouch.

Festival de Dakar
p—CNRS/CFE. *d*—Jean Rouch.

1965   **La goumbé des jeunes noceurs** (The goumbe of young revellers)
p—CNRS and Films de la Pléiade, Paris. *d*—Jean Rouch.
35/16mm—colour—30 mins.
Film about a goumbé society formed by migrants in Treichville as a focus for social activity amongst people living away from their homes and the traditional kinship structure. The film features the society's members both at work and when involved in the goumbé activities, culminating in a large open air dance.

Hampi
p—CNRS/CFE. *d*—Jean Rouch.
16mm—colour—25 mins.
A ritual vase, the Hampi, is placed in the centre of the open air museum at the Republic of Niger at Niamey, in the course of a ritual ceremony during which the dances of possession are performed.

Musique et danse des chasseurs Gow (Music and dances of the Gow hunters)
p—CNRS/CFE. *d*—Jean Rouch.
16mm—colour—20 mins.

The film brings together different elements of ritual music of the Gow hunters of the Niger, recorded during the filming of *Lion hunting with bow and arrow*. Players of portable drums; stories and mimes of the hunters returning from an expedition.

Jackville
p—CNRS/CFE. *d*—Jean Rouch.
16mm—colour—20 mins.
A Harrist ceremony in Jackville near Abidjan (Ivory Coast).

La chasse au lion à l'arc (The lion hunters)
p—Films de la Pléiade and CNRS. *d, ph*—Jean Rouch in collaboration with Damouré Zika, Ibrahim Dia, Tallou Mouzourane. *sd*—Idrissa Meiga, Moussa Alidou. *ed*—Josée Matarasse, Dov Hoenig.
The hunters—Tahirou Koro, Wangari Moussa, Belebia Hamadou, Ausseini Dembo, Sidiko Ko ro, Ali the apprentice.
35/16mm—colour—88 mins (alt. running time: 75 mins).
The film was made on the Niger/Mali border during seven periods of research, funded by CNRS and IFAN (Niger) from 1957–1965. Released June 1967. Prix Lion d'Or at Venice in 1965. The script was published in *L'Avant-Scène du Cinéma*, no. 107, October 1970.

A chronicle, filmed over seven years, of all the technological aspects of lion hunting: making bows, making poison, traps, the hunt and its attendant ritual etc. But unlike 'classic' ethnographic films dealing with hunting technology (e.g. Dunlop's films on the Aborigines or Balicki's Netsilik Eskimo series) this film also deals with the relationships between hunters and prey, and also inscribes the effect of the hunt on Rouch, and his involvement in it. As a document it is both personal and ethnographic.

Shot with an old Bell and Howell which allowed for 20 second shots and little camera movement. Some of the early sections of the film were shot silent and, unusual for Rouch, there is some soundtrack music. On the whole it is in Rouch's subjective and 'poetic' commentary that he foregrounds his own involvement, although there is an inserted section showing the telegram sent by the hunters to Rouch asking him to return as the hunt was about to re-commence. In this film we see a continuation of Rouch's attempts to construct a more 'participatory cinema', a 'shared anthropology' as well as a way of documenting disappearing practices: the commentary is addressed to children who will not be able to be hunters themselves in the future.

The film also raises questions of morality in relation to documentary film practice: at one point in the film a shepherd is attacked and badly mauled by a lion; Rouch stopped filming (although the sound man carried on recording) as he felt in some ways responsible for the shepherd's presence. The man had got into that situation because the film makers felt intrigued as to how he would use a camera to trap a lion. Rouch has said that if the man had died he would not have shown the film.

Interview in *Cahiers du Cinéma*, no. 156, June 1965, with Claude Lévi-Strauss on his interest in the cinema, conducted by Michel Delahaye and Jacques Rivette, during which Lévi-Strauss talked briefly about Rouch and cinéma vérité. In this interview he stated that whilst admiring the ethnographic documentaries of Rouch, he thought that the fiction films such as *Moi, un noir* and *La pyramide humaine* were a long way from the truth. For Rouch, cinéma-vérité is granted the same status as 'the notebooks of the ethnographer or sociologist working in the field. Only we don't publish our notebooks: they are for our own use.' Cinema vérité can never be the truth as 'it becomes necessary to transform truth into a spectacle . . . because that truth, taken by itself, would be too annoying and no one would consent to watch it.' So it is clear that for Lévi-Strauss there is a clear distinction between the ethnographic documentary and the fiction film, and that as far as a fiction film is concerned, 'it would probably be better made with professionals, a scenario and *mise en scène*'.

1966 **Batteries Dogon—éléments pour une étude des rythmes** (Drums of the Dogon—elements for a study of rhythms)
p—CNRS/CFE. *d*—Jean Rouch with Gilbert Rouget.
16mm—colour—25 mins.
Film of the young goatherds of the cliff of Bandiagara in Mali, beating different rhythms on stone drums, wooden drums and drums with skins.

Fêtes de novembre à Bregbo (November festival at Bregbo)
p—CNRS/CFE. *d*—Jean Rouch.
16mm—colour—25 mins.
Film of the festival of the Harris sect, with whom Rouch had filmed *Monsieur Albert, Prophète*, at Bregbo in the Ivory Coast.

Dongo Horendi
p—CNRS/CFE. *d*—Jean Rouch.
16mm—colour—30 mins.
Initiation to the dance of possession of a new 'Dongo horse' (the thunder divinity). Each day, the initiate, Dyomanci, dressed as a woman, is taught the dance steps which lead to possession. On the last day, he receives the ritual costumes, the objects of Dongo, and the priests' advice. Several days later, Dyomanci is questioned on the meaning he gives to the initiation.

Dongo Yenendi
p—CNRS/CFE. *d*—Jean Rouch.
16mm—colour—45 mins.
Rainmaking rites. A first attempt at film portrait of a Songhay divinity, Dongo, the thunder spirit.

Koli Koli
p—CNRS/CFE. *d*—Jean Rouch.
16mm—colour—30 mins.
Young Gow hunters in the region of Yatakalla (Niger) go hunting with dogs. Preparing and using guinea-fowl traps. 'Fakarey' tales (conversation proverbs) told by the young hunters when the hunt is over.

Sigui année zero (Sigui year zero)
p—CNRS/CFE. *d*—Jean Rouch and G. Dieterlen.
16mm—colour—50 mins.
The religious leader of all the Dogon of the Bandiagara cliff (Mali) announces the opening of the Sigui for the coming year. In the village of

You, where the ceremonies begin, the old people talk about omens and the messages they will have to send to the young people of the plain or those who work in Ghana and the Ivory Coast.

The first of eight films by Rouch in collaboration with the ethnographer Germaine Dieterlen. Sigui is the name of a cycle of ritual festivals taking place among the Dogon of the cliff of Bandiagara every sixty years. The cycle lasted eight years (1966–73).

Article by Rouch in *Filmrutan*, no. 1, entitled *Afrika Vaknar* [Wake up Africa].

1967   **Jaguar**
p—Films de la Pléiade, Paris. *d*—Jean Rouch. *Scenario*—improvised during shooting.
Cast (non-professional actors): Damouré Zika, Lam Ibrahim Dia, Illo Gaoudel.
16mm—colour—110 mins.
Made between 1954–67; first shown in 1971. When Rouch had brought the early rushes of *Jaguar* to Paris at the same time as *Mammy Water* and *Les maîtres fous*, Pierre Braunberger (of Films de la Pléiade) was only interested in the latter, and Rouch had no money of his own to make a copy. Later Gerard Philipe, to whom the final film is dedicated, provided money for a copy. Rouch returned to Ghana in 1956–7 with this copy, showed it to Damouré and Lam who together improvised the commentary in much the same manner as that of *Moi, un noir*. Many of the sequences in the final film were shot at this time (using, incidentally, the same Bell and Howell used for *Moi, un noir*). This was the period of Nkrumah's premiership, shortly after Ghana's independence and Rouch sees the main interest of the film today as being 'a witnessing of that revolutionary period'. Since then the kind of migrations which form the basis of the film's rambling and picaresque story have been stopped in West Africa. The different episodes of the film were worked out by the actors at the time of shooting. Rouch describes the film as 'pure fiction': 'It was a banal story. A series of banal adventures which happened to these people in a world which was perfectly strange to them'. Further conversations were recorded in 1967 and the final soundtrack is a 'sound-montage' of these and the earlier recordings. Rouch showed a version of $2\frac{1}{2}$ hrs at the Cinémathèque, a version which apparently survives in a black and white print with himself improvising the commentary. But the release print was cut to approximately 110 mins. Rouch: 'For me it's a little like surrealist painting: using the realest possible products of reproduction . . . in the service of the unreal, putting them in the presence of irrational elements. A post-card in the service of the imaginary'. 'Jaguar' is the West African term for a sophisticated townboy.

Dauda Sorko
p—CNRS/CFE. *d*-Jean Rouch.
16mm—colour—15 mins.
Film of Dauda, the high priest of the thunder-god, telling Damouré Zika the myth of Dongo and the seven Tourou, the highest gods of Songhay mythology.

22

Sigui: l'enclume de Yougo (The Anvil of Yougo)
p—CNRS/CFE. *d*—Jean Rouch.
16mm—colour—50 mins.
Beginning of the sextenary festival of the Sigui among the Dogon of the Bandiagara cliff. After the brewing of the beer and the making of the decorations and costumes, the men, shaved and dressed in the ritual clothes of the Sigui, enter the public square dancing the snake dance. They honour the terraces of the famous dead of the last sixty years and go on to drink the sacramental millet beer. Then they go off in procession carrying the Sigui to other Sigui villages. It will return to its starting point in seven years' time.

Tourou et Bitti
p—CNRS/CFE. *d*—Jean Rouch, assisted by Lam Ibrahim Dia and Tallou Mouzourane. *sd*—Moussa Hamidou.
16mm—colour—8 mins.
Other filmographies, including those by G. Marsolais and *Filmkritik*, list this film as produced in 1971.

Hailed as an example of participatory cinema, in which the camera is perfectly integrated with the pro-filmic event. 'In this short film, lasting the length of one magazine, the camera is registering dances preparatory to a possession—which does not happen. After a few minutes the rhythm of the music and the dance slows down, finally stopping altogether. The musicians then turn towards the camera, and, noticing that Jean Rouch is still filming (he had begun to film expressly to catch the phenomenon of the possession which he believed was about to be produced) they begin to beat on the calabasses with an accelerated rhythm. So much so that the dance is taken up again simultaneously and . . . the phenomenon of the possession is produced! Something which would evidently not have happened if Rouch had stopped filming. This remarkable document permits us to realise that not only is Jean Rouch (and his camera) accepted by the people to the point of not really being noticed, but also that, because he has known the people of Niger for over twenty-five years, he is accepted by them to the point of being considered as the equal of an officiant (priest) during a ceremony and of exercising a certain influence over its development.' (G. Marsolais, p. 180). The film is described by Rouch in the voice-over commentary as 'ethnographic cinema in the first person'.

Publication of the UNESCO *Catalogue des Films Ethnographiques sur l'Afrique Noire*, prepared by the Comité du Film Ethnographique of the CNRS. The preface and an essay entitled *Situation et Tendances du Cinéma en Afrique* were written by Rouch.

Article on direct cinema and interview with Rouch by James Blue in *Film Comment*, vol. 4, nos 2/3.

Interview about *Jaguar* in *Cahiers du Cinéma*, no. 195.

1968   Yenendi de Ganghel
p—CNRS/CFE. *d*—Jean Rouch.
16mm—colour—60 mins.
In August 1968, lightning struck a small village of newly settled fishermen at Ganghel near Niamey (Niger). The Zima priests and the Sorko fishermen organised on the village square a 'Yenendi', ceremony of purifi-

cation, in the course of which Dongo, the divinity of thunder and his brothers, summoned by the calabash drummers and the violins, possess their horses.

Pierres chantantes d'Ayorou (Singing stones of Ayorou)
p—CNRS/CFE. *d*—Jean Rouch.
16mm—colour—10 mins.
On the Island of Ayorou (Niger), Tondi tyi Harey, a huge block pierced with small holes is a 'singing stone'. The children come there to put rhythm into new tunes, the goumbés, sometimes to the sound of guitars.

Wanzerbe
p—CNRS/CFE. *d*—Jean Rouch.
16mm—colour—20 mins.
A dance of possession is organised to designate the successor to the head of the magicians of Wanzerbe who has just died. But the divinities have only just appeared when the daughter of the proposed high priest dies in labour. Kassey, 'woman chief' of the magicians of Wanzerbe, has expressed her disapproval.

Sigui 1968—Les danceurs de Tyogou (The dancers of Tyogou)
p—CNRS/CFE. *d*—Jean Rouch with G. Dieterlen.
16mm—colour—50 mins.
Second year of the sextenary festival of the Sigui among the Dogon of the Bandiagara cliff. In the village of Tyogou, the men prepare head-dresses and decorations of Sigui. Then they leave in procession for the sites of former villages and come back to dance on the public square and drink millet beer. The next day they decorate the cave of the masks where the new great masks will be brought at the end of the ceremonies.

Un lion nommé l'Americain (A lion called 'The American')
p—CNRS and Films de la Pleïade, Paris. *d*—Jean Rouch.
35/16mm—colour—20 mins.
Sequel to *La chasse au lion à l'arc*, 'The American' was the name of a particularly ferocious lion that the hunters had wounded but not caught in the previous film.

The following is a montage of statements by Rouch on the events of May '68. (For a fuller background to these events, see Sylvia Harvey, *May '68 and Film Culture*, BFI 1978.)

'It is necessary to know the reasons for a certain failure in the month of May. For example, for me, in the month of May the position of the cinema was simple. It was necessary to demand a laboratory to develop the films which were made at that time and it was necessary to occupy one or more cinemas to show every day the rushes of the day before. It was also necessary to occupy the Centre du Cinéma so that in the future none of these situations would happen again.

Cinéthique interviewer: 'It was necessary to occupy television as well, but that wasn't done.'
Rouch: 'Why wasn't it done? Because in the domain of cinema the people involved are either capitalists or old trade union militants who were

defending their prerogatives. At that time it seemed difficult to me to do anything as it was a period of active repression. It was easy to pass into illegality . . . It is necessary that there are clandestine movements, but also that there are people who are continuing the movement in the old system, who permit the development of new techniques.' *Cinéthique*, no. 3, March 1969 (Trans. M.R.E.).

'. . . Godard was incapable of making a film in '68. I too was incapable maybe because I was doing other things. Film was in the street and it was not worth making. One had to *live* it. There is not one good book on '68. Cohn-Bendit's book is not valid. The only valid book is by the chief of the Paris police who tells everything that took place. He was confused by May '68. He was completely in agreement with Cohn-Bendit and the others. This is wonderful but it's sad it is the only one. All the people who participated, sociologists like Touraine, Edgar Morin, all were incapable of saying anything about it.' *Film Quarterly*, vol. 31, no. 3, spring 1978. Morin's book referred to is *Mai 68—La Brèche*, written with Claude Lefort and Jean-Marc Coudray, Fayard, Paris 1968.

'For me the events of May '68 represented the awareness of the danger which is lying in wait for our society. I learnt in school that societies die like people. It's possible that we're coming to the end of our industrial society which will be replaced by something else. That doesn't mean we will go back to using bicycles and roller skates and bows and arrows, but to a different conception of life. Actually it is certain that in the areas that I know (I don't know them all) the ways of life which are offered to the young are intolerable. I am not saying that a return to nature is the solution but I do think a certain reflection is necessary. I reject a civilisation of robots and cosmonauts, of a 'pentagonal' bureaucracy. Let us say that my proposal is not to throw bombs, but to light fire-crackers.' *Cinema 3*, (Morocco), no. 1, January 1970. (Trans. M.R.E.)

Substantial article about Rouch in *Cahiers du Cinéma*, nos. 200–201.

Article by Rouch, *Le film ethnographique* in *Ethnologie Générale—Encyclopédie de la Pleïade*, Eds. Gallimard, Paris.

1969   **Petit à Petit** (Little by Little)
p—Films de la Pleïade, Paris. *d, ph*—Jean Rouch. *Assistant*—Phillipe Luzuy. *sd*—Moustapha Hamidou. *ed*—Josée Matarasso, Dominique Villain.

Cast (non-professional actors): Damouré Zika, Lam Ibrahim Dia, Illo Gaoudel, Safi Faye, Ariane Bruneton, Phillippe Luzuy, Tallou Mouzourane, Moustapha Alassane, Idrissa Maiga, Marie, Alborah Maiga, Charles Chabord, Michel Delahaye, Sylvie Pierre, Patricia Finaly, Zomo and his brothers.

Made with the collaboration of CNRS (Niamey) and CFE (Paris). Released in September 1971.

16mm—colour—105 mins (alt. running time: $4\frac{1}{2}$ hrs)

The script of the film was published in *L'Avant-Scène du Cinéma*, no. 123, March 1972.

This film is a sequel to *Jaguar*. At the end of that film, Damouré and Lam had founded a company known as 'Petit à Petit' from the proverb: 'little by little the bird makes his bonnet'—the bonnet being the turban of a chief. In this film the company has prospered and Damouré is sent to Paris to see how people live there on the occasion of a skyscraper being built in the Ivory Coast.

Rouch: 'The idea of my film is to transform anthropology, the eldest daughter of colonialism, a discipline reserved to those with power interrogating people without it. I want to replace it by a shared anthropology. That is to say, an anthropological dialogue between people belonging to different cultures, which for me represents the discipline of human sciences for the future.' (*Le Monde,* 16 June, 1971.)

Filmed in September–October 1968 in Paris and the early months of 1969 in Africa. One year of editing produced two versions, one of 4½ hrs and another of 105 mins for general release, cut from 6 hrs of material mostly composed of ten minute sequence shots. Rouch has said the film would have been very different if it had been made before the events of May '68. By this he seems to imply, not that the construction of film altered because of those events as much as the fact that its impact would have been different had those events not taken place, as the 'naive objections' that Damouré puts to the consumer society would have had a different value before '68.

The film develops many of Rouch's recurring preoccupations: the creation of a 'reality' by starting from fiction, the confrontation between blacks and whites, although this time in Europe and not in Africa, and the development of a 'shared anthropology'.

Sigui 1969—La caverne de Bongo (Sigui 1969—the Bongo cave)
p—CNRS/CFE. *d*—Jean Rouch with G. Dieterlen.
16mm—colour—40 mins.
Third year of the sextenary ceremonies of the Sigui among the Dogon from the Bandiagara cliff. The Olou Barou dignitaries finish their retreat in the Bongo cave. Around the old Anai, dean of the ceremony, who will see his third Sigui (he is therefore more than 120 years old) the men shave and share salt and sesame. They paint in red and white the altar which will be the centre of the ceremony. Then dressed in cowrie shoulder belts they make a tour of the lineage area before drinking the sacramental beer.

Article on the ideology of direct cinema and the use of its techniques in fiction films, *Le détour par le direct,* by Jean-Louis Comolli in *Cahiers du Cinéma,* nos. 209 and 211, February and April 1969.

Un terrorisme économique: Interview with Rouch on cinema technology and the events of May '68, in *Cinéthique,* no. 3, March 1969.

1970   **Yenendi de Yantalla**
p—CNRS/CFE. *d*—Jean Rouch.
16mm—colour—30 mins.
In May, at Yantalla, a district of Niamey, the priests call on Dongo and his brothers to ask them for more rain and less thunder than in previous years. The gods are reticent about appearing (several processions fail) and reticent in answering. The year will be a bad one.

Mya—la mère (Mya—the mother)
p—CNRS/CFE. *d*—Jean Rouch.
16mm—colour—12 mins.
Short film of an African mother suckling her two year old child.

Sigui 1970—Les clameurs d'Amani (Sigui 1970—the clamour of Amani)
p—CNRS-CFE. *d*—Jean Rouch with G. Dieterlen.
16mm—colour—50 mins.
Fourth year of the sextenary ceremonies of the Sigui among the Dogon of the Bandiagara cliff. The 'Pale Fox' is questioned by the headman of Bongo and shows him the road taken by the Sigui of Amani. With the elders and the drums in front, the men of Sigui begin a procession which winds its way deviously through the village before coming to the place of ritual.

Interview in *Cinema 3*, no. 1 (Morocco).

1971 **Porto Novo—La danse des reines** (Port Novo—dance of the queens)
p—CNRS/CFE. *d*—Jean Rouch with Gilbert Rouget.
16mm—colour—30 mins.
Ritual dancing of the queens of the Royal Palace of Porto Novo in Dahomey. The technique of slow motion with synchronised sound allows for analysis of the relationships between music and dance.

Sigui 1971—La dune d'Idyeli (Sigui 971—the dune of Idyeli)
p—CNRS/CFE. *d*—Jean Rouch with G. Dieterlen.
16mm—colour—50 mins.
Fifth year of the sextenary ceremonies of the Sigui among the Dogon of the Bandiagara cliff. The arrival of the Sigui in the village of Idyeli. In the night the rhombs call the men of the village to the last retreat. The next day the men come down again to the village and go in procession to the public square where they dance and sing for two days.

Architects Ayorou (Ayorou architects)
p—CNRS/CFE. *d*—Jean Rouch.
16mm—colour—30 mins.
Traditional houses and new architecture in Ayorou, an island on the river Niger in the archipelago of Tillaberi. The houses; grinding millet; a newly-wedded young man's house is being built.

Yenendi de Simiri (Yenendi of Simiri)
p—CNRS/CFE. *d*—Jean Rouch.
16mm—colour—30 mins.
After three years of drought, the peasants of the Simiri region (Niger) question the sky gods, responsible for rain. The gods answer evasively blaming it on their having abandoned the old customs.

Long interview, *Jean Rouch ou les aventures d'un nègre blanc*, conducted by Philippe Esnault in *Image et Son*, no. 249, April 1971.

Other interviews in *Filme Cultura* (Brasil), no. 15; *Cinema 71*, no. 160; *Téléciné*, no. 174 and *Hablemos de cinema*, nos 61–62.

Publication of *Documentary Explorations* by G. Roy Levin, Doubleday Anchor, New York, including a long interview with Rouch conducted in 1969.

Publication of *Dziga Vertov* by Georges Sadoul, eds. Champ Libre, Paris, with a short preface by Jean Rouch, entitled *Cinq Regards sur Vertov* [Five looks at Vertov].

1972   **Funérailles du vieil Anai** (Funeral of the old Anai)
p—CNRS/CFE. *d*—Jean Rouch with Germaine Dieterlen.
16mm—colour—45 mins (alt. running time 90 mins).
The oldest inhabitant of the village of Bongo (Mali) died aged 122. He was head of the society of the masks. Men come from neighbouring villages to take part in mock battles with flintlock guns, spears and bows. The great mask of Bongo prepared during the ceremony of Sigui 1969 is put up in front of the cavern of the masks. Men and women of Bongo recite ritual mottos of old Anai and dance and weep.

An unedited version, running 90 mins was first shown publicly in April 1979 as part of a programme organised by *Cahiers du Cinéma*.

Horendi
p—CNRS/CFE. *d*—Jean Rouch.
16mm—colour—30 mins.
An attempt to analyse the relationships between dance and music in the course of a ceremony of initiation to the dance of possession (certain sequences are filmed in slow motion with synchronised sound). Two women, possessed by Kirey, the divinity of lightning are present during the seven days of initiation.

Sigui 1972—Les pagnes de Iame (The loincloths of Iame)
p—CNRS/CFE. *d*—Jean Rouch with G. Dieterlen.
16mm—colour—50 mins.
Sixth year of the sextenary ceremonies of the Sigui in the village of Iame. Village scenes, preparation of the ritual seats. In the bush, the men put on their ornaments and then come into the village to drink the millet beer. The dignitaries carry symbolically the Sigui towards the West where it will take place the following year.

Yenendi de Boukoki
p—CNRS/CFE. *d*—Jean Rouch.
16mm—colour—25 mins.
Annual festival of the Yenendi in the new district of Boukoki in Niamey (Niger). Around the 'hampi', the vase of the sky, Dongo, the thunder divinity, and his brothers are possessed. With the help of the Hauka divinities, they put out a fire of straw symbolising the bush fires, and foretell what the next rainy season will be like.

Tanda Singui
p—CNRS/CFE. *d*—Jean Rouch.
16mm—colour—30 mins.
The inhabitants of the Yantalla district in Niamey build a 'shed' (place for the possession cult) for the thunder divinity, Dongo. A series of shots show successively the possession of Zakao (the slave of Dongo), of Dongo himself and of Harakoy (the water divinity, mother of Dongo). After the sacrifice of a he-goat, the ritual musicians play on the new shed.

Interview in *L'Avant Scène du Cinéma*, no. 123.

1973   **L'Enterrement du Hogon** (The burial of the Hogon)
p—CNRS/CFE. *d*—Jean Rouch.
16mm—colour—15 mins.
Burial of the Hogon, religious leader of the Sanga region (Mali). The
hunter-warriors assemble round the deceased leader's hut and simulate a
battle using guns, spears or millet stalks. Various rites are performed. The
body is carried away and placed in the cave used as burial ground.

VW-Voyou
p—SCOA. *d*—Jean Rouch.
16mm—colour—30 mins.
Advertising film designed to show that the VW is the perfect car for
African road conditions. Damouré Zika plays a variety of roles (a
shepherd, a business man, a hunter, a doctor) and the film is broadly
comical through its use of 'primitive' cinematic effects such as playing the
film backwards, stopframe photography etc. According to the German
magazine *Filmkritik*, 'The film was not named as being by J. R. by the
agency, as he was considered "too destructive".'

Dongo Hori
p—CNRS/CFE. *d*—Jean Rouch.
16mm—colour—20 mins.
In a new district of Niamey (Niger), an old Zima woman 'horse' of the
thunder divinity Dongo, organises a festival to thank the master of the sky
for rain received and to ask for more.

Sécheresse à Simiri (Drought at Simiri)
p—CNRS/CFE. *d*—Jean Rouch.
16mm—colour—30 mins.
Despite the ritual of rain of Yenendi in the month of May, the rainfall is
insufficient and in the course of the month of August, Dongo, the thunder
divinity, strikes a tree in the middle of the village. Despite a new purification ritual, the harvest is bad and the farmers and priests put the blame
on their not respecting 'the true tradition'.

Boukoki
p—CNRS/CFE. *d*—Jean Rouch.
16mm—colour—10 mins.
Rain ritual in the seventh month of the dry season in a suburb of Niamey
(Niger). The sky gods 'possessing' their horses produce the year's rainfall.

Hommage à Marcel Mauss: Taro Okamoto
p—CNRS/CFE. *d*—Jean Rouch.
16mm—colour—14 mins.
Interview with the sculptor Taro Okamoto in his studio in Tokyo.
Okamoto had been Mauss' student in Paris from 1930 to 1939.
    Publication of *Jean Rouch* by Gilles Marsolais, Cinémathèque
Quebeçoise, January 1973, to coincide with a series of lectures given by
Rouch at the University of Montreal.

International Conference on Visual Anthropology held in Chicago, where Rouch contributed a paper, *The Camera and Man* (extracts are reprinted in this monograph). The papers prepared for this conference were reprinted in *Principles of Visual Anthropology*, ed. Paul Hockings, Mouton, the Hague 1975. For a critical review of this, see *Anthropology and Film* by M. Eaton and I. Ward in *Screen*, vol. 17, no. 3, autumn 1976.

1974   **Cocorico, Monsieur Poulet** (Cock-a-doodle, Mister Hen)
p—IRSH (Niamey)/CRNS and Secr. d'État à la Coopération (Paris), *d*—Dalarou (i.e. Damouré Zika, Lam Ibrahim Dia and Jean Rouch). *ph*—Jean Rouch. *sd*—Moussa Hamidou and Hama Soumana. *ed*—Christine Lefort. *Music*—Tallou Mouzourane.
Cast (non-professional actors): Damouré Zika, Lam Ibrahim Dia, Tallou Mouzourane, Claudine, Sadia Nore, Moussa Illo.
16mm—colour—90 mins.
Picaresque story of three friends and an old sorceress who travel through the bush selling chickens in an old 2CV, the film is 'an attempt at collective improvisation on a popular folktale from Niger—focusing on the life styles and attitudes of African marginals or drop outs.' (*Cineaste*, vol. 8, no. 4, summer 1978). A fiction film composed, once again, of ten minute sequence shots with very little editing.
    Rouch: 'I have come to the conclusion that changes in society are due primarily to people who are on the fringes of society, those who see the economic absurdity of the system. I regard them as a kind of populist avant-garde.'
    The film opened commercially in Paris, but the distributor went bankrupt and the 35mm prints were confiscated by the receiver. More material can be found in the *Cineaste* interview quoted above, entitled *The Politics of Visual Anthropology*. The interview was conducted by Dan Georgakas, Udayan Gupta and Judy Janda.

Pam Kuso Kar (*Briser les potteries de Pam*) (Breaking Pam's vases)
p—CNRS/CFE. *d*—Jean Rouch.
16mm—colour—10 mins.
In February 1974, Pam Sambo Zima, oldest of the possession priests in Niamey (Niger) died over 70 years old. In the yard of his lot, the faithful of the possession cult 'break' symbolically the dead priest's ritual vases and weep for the deceased while sharing out the clothes of the divinities.

Sigui 1973—L'auvent de la circoncision (The circumcision shelter)
p—CNRS/CFE. *d*—Jean Rouch.
16mm—colour—15 mins.
This film, shot in 1974, is a reconstitution of the simple ending ceremony which marked the seventh and last year of the sextenary ceremonies of the Sigui in 1972. Filming was forbidden in Mali in 1972 because of the drought.

La 504 et les foudroyers (The Peugeot 504 and the bolts of lightning)
p—SCOA. *d*—Jean Rouch with Damouré and Lam.
16mm—colour—10 mins.

Advertising film showing a Peugeot 504 being tested in the rocky region of Bandiagara in Mali. It drives on roads which have been blown up by the 'lightning throwers'.

Ambara Dama
p—CNRS/CFE. d—Jean Rouch with Germaine Dieterlen.
16mm—colour—60 mins.
Ambara, one of the Griaule team's principal informants among the Dogon from Bandiagara, is dead. During the following year, the Sanga Society of masks organises a Grand Dama, ceremony in which all the old masks are replaced by new ones. A similar ceremony had been watched by Griaule forty years before. Slow motion synchronised sound has been used to study the dances of the masks.

Sécheresse à Simiri
p—CNRS/CFE. d—Jean Rouch.
16mm—colour—10 mins.
Continuation of the film of the same name of 1973.

Toboy Tobaye (*Lapin, petit lapin*) (Rabbit, little rabbit)
p—CNRS/CFE. d—Jean Rouch.
16mm—colour—12 mins.
Dances of today and yesterday by children disguised as rabbits during the nights of fasting in Ramadan (Niger).
   Publication of *L'Aventure du Cinéma Direct* by Gilles Marsolais, Cinéma club, Editions Seghers, Paris. A comprehensive account of the history, theory and practices of direct cinema.

1975   **Souna Kouma** (*La nostalgie de Souna*) (Nostalgia of Souna)
p—CNRS/CFE. d—Jean Rouch.
16mm—colour—30 mins.
Funeral ritual for a deceased priest in Niamey (Niger) in January 1975. Purification of the 'horses' which he had initiated; the gods choose his successor.

Initiation
p—CNRS/CFE. d—Jean Rouch.
16mm—colour—45 mins.
Initiation ritual of a young woman who is possessed by Kirey, the god of lightning.
   Interview in *La Nouvelle Critique*, no. 82.

1976   **Babatou ou les trois conseils** (Babatou or the three pieces of advice)
p—CNRS/CFE. d—Jean Rouch and Boubou Hama.
16mm—colour—90 mins.
A film based on the chronicles of the slave war of Babatou who attacked and conquered the Songhay in Gurunsiland, and the re-telling of a fairy tale in which the morality of the figures is reflected. Made for £30,000.
   Rouch: 'It is historical fiction, a very ambitious film because it is fiction on history. It is a very subjective film in which the story is told in two

different ways that are both false. The truth will never be told, especially when it is a story of war . . . I think it is difficult to make such a film. It was very controversial in Africa because it shows that African wars were ridiculous. In fact when I shot it, I thought a lot about Godard's *Les Carabiniers* . . . The film shows what could happen in a war of slavery in which there were no dead. We show the war as a sort of sports tournament, as words and insults rather than action. The epic account that people make, the oral tradition—the minstrels—is completely false'. (From an interview with Dan Yakir in *Film Quarterly*, vol. 31, no. 3, spring 1978.)

Médecines et médecins (Medicines and doctors)
p—CFE and the Institut de Recherches en Sciences Humaines (Niamey). *d*—Jean Rouch with Ousseini.
16mm—colour—15 mins.
Retired nurses of Niger practice surgery on market places and call on local healers for post-operative care.

Rythme de Travail (Work rhythm)
p—CNRS/CFE. *d*—Jean Rouch.
16mm—colour—12 mins.
Collective improvisation singing while grinding millet; a peasant chant and a profane dance after a failed possession dance.

1977 **Makwayela**
p—CNRS/CFE and the Institut Mocambicaen de Cinema. *d*—Jean Rouch.
16mm—colour—20 mins.
Rouch: 'I have just returned from Mozambique where I went at the invitation of the Film Institute to present a few films and work with some local directors. I think my visit shook them up a bit, as I urged them not to make films about party congresses—to get out of official cinema. Together we made a film which is a kind of follow up to *Come Back Africa* by Lionel Rogosin: on the workers of Mozambique who return to their country (from working in the mines of South Africa—Ed.) in song and dance. I think I showed that creativity is everywhere and one could make films like this, that one should continually fight against conformism, against accepted ideas, and that it is necessary to stir up people. If I play a little role in African cinema, this is it. Even if my films are censored and criticised.' (*Film Quarterly*, interview, *op. cit.*)

Ciné-Portrait de Margaret Mead
p—CFE and Museum of Natural History, New York. *d*—Jean Rouch.
sd—John Marshall.
16mm—colour—35 mins.
Rouch: 'For me, documentary and fiction are similar. For example, I plan to make a film on Margaret Mead. For me, she is what we call in anthropology a 'totemic ancestor', so we're already in the imaginary. I know that with the camera, when we have a dialogue, it'll be a fiction film on the world, the US, what we think, our dreams etc. I'll provoke her with

32

the camera, interview her and be the cameraman all at once. And we'll shoot for ten minutes or so until we're tired'. (*Film Quarterly* interview, *op. cit.*)

Filmed in September 1977 at the Museum of Natural History in New York, where Mead kept an office since the twenties, the film is a benevolent portrait of someone who is not only a 'totemic ancestor' in relation to the discipline of anthropology, but also, through her work with Gregory Bateson in Bali, an early advocate of the use of film in the practice of ethnographic research as a 'note taking tool'. During the interview Mead talks of her first experience of field-work, her subsequent visits to Manos and Bali, and the importance of anthropology in building new cultures of the future.

Isphahan: Lettre Persane *1977* (La Mosquée du Chah à Isfahan)
p—CNRS/CFE. *d*—Jean Rouch.
16mm—colour—35 mins.
Interview (in four long sequence shots) with F. Gaffary in the royal mosque at Isfahan on the filmic representation of Islam, on sex and death.

Fête des Gandyi Bi à Simiri
p—CNRS/CFE. *d*—Jean Rouch.
16mm—colour—30 mins.
The last ceremony presided over by the Zima Siddo—peasants of a village in Niger ask the god of the jungle for protection against predatory animals. The gods intimate that the Zima Siddo will die that year.

Le Griot Badye (Badye, the minstrel)
p—CNRS/CFE. *d*—Jean Rouch with Ousseini.
16mm—colour—15 mins.
A traditional singer using birdsong as a source for the music he uses to accompany his story telling.

Hommage à Marcel Mauss: Marcel Levy
p—CNRS/CFE. *d*—Jean Rouch.
16mm—colour—20 mins.
Interview with Sociologist and theologian Marcel Levy.

Hommage à Marcel Mauss: Germaine Dieterlen
p—CNRS/CFE. *d*—Jean Rouch.
16mm—colour—20 mins.
Interview with the ethnologist and collaborator of Rouch.
    Interviews published in *Ecran*, no. 56, and *Skoop*, no. 5.

1978   Jean Rouch and his camera in the heart of Africa
p—NOS Television, Hilversum. *d*—Philo Bregstein. *ph*—Djingarei Maiga, Jean Rouch, Ricardo de Silva. *sd*—Amadou Soumana, Moussa Illo, Michel Allencraz. *Music*—Tallo Mouzarane. *ed*—Hans van Dongen.
A filmed portrait of Rouch, made for TV, dealing with his work in Africa and his influence on ethnographic film.

Simiri Siddo Kuma
p—CNRS/CFE. *d*—Jean Rouch.
16mm—colour—30 mins.
Funeral of the Zima Siddo and appointment by the gods of his successor.
Interviews in *Film Quarterly*, vol. 31, no. 3, and *Cineaste*, vol. 8, no. 4.
Dossier on cinema-vérité in *On Film*, no. 8. *Filmkritik*, no. 253, devoted to
Jean Rouch, includes an article by the director.

1979   17–25 March: Cinéma du Réel, an international festival of ethnographic
film held at the Georges Pompidou Centre in Paris. Rouch served on the
organising committee. Films shown included Rouch's portrait of Margaret
Mead, and the film made by Philo Bregstein for Dutch TV.

The magazine *Framework* prepares the publication of a translation of
Rouch's preface to the book on Vertov and of Rouch's lecture on
Rossellini. To be published in *Framework* no. 11.

Special screenings of Rouch's work at the Edinburgh Film Festival.

Currently, Rouch is involved in the European distribution of African
films.

DIRECT

Michel Marie

Editorial note: *This article is included in this monograph as a supplement to the technological information on the development of sync-sound contained in the previous section. The importance of this short article lies in Marie's contextualisation of direct cinema as a practice which foregrounds the crucial function of sound in film and in his refusal to see direct cinema simply as a means of capturing reality directly.*

The article first appeared in Lectures du film, *Eds Albatros, Paris 1976, and this translation by Fabrice Ziolkowski was published in the American Magazine* On Film, *no. 8, spring 1978.*

The concept of 'direct cinema' designates first of all a new technique of recording pro-filmic reality. This term which replaced the more ambiguous 'cinema vérité' at the beginning of the sixties applies, beyond a simple technique, to a whole current which overthrew methods of film making previously completely standardised through the industrial model. To this technique corresponds an aesthetic based on a return to the primordial function of spoken language and the 'direct and authentic contact' with 'lived' reality. This aesthetic is, of course, the product of a neo-naturalist ideology, a dominant one in the 'new cinema' of the sixties. The technical, aesthetic and ideological consequences of direct cinema are rather considerable and are still developing.

1. A new technique

In the technical sense of the term, 'direct' designates the synchronous recording of image and sound. This sound recorded directly is not, like the sound of an industrial production, a 'witnessing sound', but the real sound of the film and will not be complemented with sound effects or post-synchronised in a studio. Sounds and images are therefore caught simultaneously and restituted in the same manner at the time of projection. But 'direct' designates also and above all the simultaneity of the shooting and of the event represented.

As opposed to industrial cinema, fictional and spectacular, in the case of direct cinema the action to be filmed is void of an anterior status. This action is therefore not pre-structured, rehearsed, etc. but it is the act of filming itself that creates the filmic event. Direct is essentially used in one format: 16mm. Its appearance as a new method of shooting dates first of all from the massive use of this format by television for certain specific categories of programmes: news reporting, documentaries, dramas, youth activities, educational television, image research and finally variety programs. Aside from television, it is used for all cinematic forms which call for light, easily handled and inexpensive equipment: reports of all sorts, scientific cinema (ethnological cinema), etc. To satisfy these different functions and to subsequently experience a certain popularity, 16mm had to resolve a few technical difficulties: the weight of the camera, the noise of its motor, the light sensitivity of its film and most of all the recording of sound, and consequently its synchronization with the image track. In the face of problems posed by the synchronous recording of sound, American technicians concentrated their efforts on perfecting the studio camera Aurican which still weighed twenty kilos with a full film load.

On their side the technicians of the Canadian Film Office worked with the German Arriflex which was still very noisy and heavy (about ten kilos with a 120 meter magazine and an additional motor). At first, light and portable soundproof bags or 'blimps' were used to lessen the noise of the motor. At the same time, shooting with synchronous sound recording and with a long lens was developed. The camera with its telephoto lens stayed far from the protagonists and their small microphones hidden in their clothing. It is mostly through the suppression of lighting problems, in the development of more sensitive stocks and their processing, that the handicaps of direct recording disappeared. Since then, with the development of the Eclair-Coutant 16mm camera and other cameras which followed this model, equipment for synchronous recording has been perfected on the technical level thanks to the use of small transistors. Working most of the time on outside energy sources, on batteries, recording equipment records sound on a normalized magnetic tape of 6.25mm which runs at a rigorously constant speed of 19.05cm per second. At the beginning of magnetic sound recording, sound-image synchronization was obtained through a wire which connected camera to tape recorder. This solution obviously had the inconvenience of limiting the movement of the camera. Since then, synchronisation of the machines is assured through quartz oscillators, which do away with the connecting wire. The use of cordless radiomicrophones brings total mobility to the recording of sound. In most cases, the sound man in direct film is equipped with a headset. He can thus listen to the sound captured by the microphone without being bothered by surrounding sounds.

These new techniques were, of course, developed for twofold reasons, an economic one (broadening of the market) and an ideological one (to 'capture life', the authentic, the real, etc.).

2. History

A teleological vision of film history would hasten to find precursors to the film makers who, in the important years of 1958–62, applied the technical methods of reporting to 'documentary' subjects. It is true that the theories of the Soviet filmmaker Dziga Vertov concerning the Kino-eye and radio-ear are echoed in the declarations and practice of direct film makers.

36

To stick with 'direct' of the years 1958–62 without going back to Lumière and Feuillade, Vertov, Flaherty, Vigo, Rouquier, etc., we can situate 'direct' historically around three principal axes: the O.N.F. (Canadian Film Board-Office National du Film), the American school and the French ethnographic cinema of Jean Rouch.

The Canadian Film Board

State organized and founded in 1939 by the Scottish documentarist John Grierson, the Canadian Film Board first turned its attention to war films. Then in 1945, it became the only organization producing several hundreds of documentaries, ethnographic and sociological films all in 16mm. It contributed to the formation of a great number of directors, technicians, cameramen, soundmen and created an animation and research section.

At first, McCartney-Filgate, initiator of the 'candid eye', wanted to liberate the camera from its tripod and to give it total freedom of movement. The idea was to find inspiration in the methods of the great photographer Cartier-Bresson and to spread them into the realm of film. The two films which are associated with the 'candid eye' are *Blood and Fire* (1958) and *Bientôt Noël* (1959), on which Wolf Koening and Michel Brault worked. We can then distinguish two different currents: one from England which will, after the departure of Filgate, develop American direct; the other from France whose principal representative is without a doubt Michel Brault. This latter current will come in contact with the French ethnographic school of Rouch. The outcome of the Canadian school of direct is the tryptich directed by Brault and Pierre Perrault: *Pour la suite du monde* (1963), *Le règne du jour* (1967) and *Les voîtures d'eau* (1969).

The American school

The American school developed under a double influence, that of the English–Canadian direct (*Lonely Boy*, 1961, directed by Koenig and Kroitor), and that of Robert Drew, journalist and producer and associate of Richard Leacock, the great cameraman who shot Flaherty's *Louisiana Story* in 1948. The first films of the Drew–Leacock team were *Primary* and *Yanki No* (1960). The new cineastes who prolonged American direct were Albert Maysles (*Showman*, 1962, *The Beatles in the U.S.A.*, 1964) and D. A. Pennebaker (*The Chair* and *Jane*, 1962, *Monterey Pop*, 1968). We can also connect to this current film makers like Shirley Clarke (*The Connection*, *The Cool World*), Robert Kramer (*The Edge, Ice*), John Cassavetes (*Shadows*, 1960, *Too Late Blues*, 1961, and most importantly *Faces*, made in 1968 and which can be considered as the most important film of this school).

French direct: Jean Rouch

Rouch is first of all an ethnologist researcher for the National Center for Scientific Research. He used the camera as early as 1947 as a recording instrument. All of his shorts between 1947 and 1954 are work documents

37

and it is the scientific use of film which must be stressed here (the shorts of the 1949–51 period have been compiled as *Les fils de l'eau*). But it is starting with *Les maîtres fous* (1954–55) that Rouch's work becomes oriented towards fiction film constructed with the methods of ethnological film. This tendency will be accentuated with *Moi, un noir* in 1957, *La pyramide humaine* in 1959 and *Chronique d'un été* in 1960. The considerable contribution of Rouch is that he provoked reflections on the question of the subject, a weak point of the Canadian school, and upset the boundaries between fiction film and document. From this point on, direct puts back into question the shooting methods of traditional cinema and it is undoubtedly Godard who first draws from Jean Rouch's teachings by shooting his films in 35mm with synchronous sound.

3. Aesthetic and ideology

A new technique responding to economic and ideological pressures, direct very quickly produced a specific aesthetic based on the relationship between film and reality. The most ambiguous aspect of this aesthetic is manifested in the term 'cinema vérité' and in the polemic which surrounded this expression. Actually, the technique of direct has allowed a whole metaphysics of reality to engulf film theory and practice. It becomes a matter of 'capturing the imponderable movement of the real', of restituting the lived in a raw manner, of eliminating any intervention from the cineaste and his or her technique, and therefore to hide, most of the time spontaneously, the work of the camera and the microphone. This evangelistic conception of the 'revelation of the authentic reality' by a contemplative camera certainly does not produce the same havoc than in the years 1962–63, but it still produces certain effects on realist and spontaneist endeavours, notably within the films produced in France during and after the months of May and June 1968.

Nonetheless, one of the undeniable contributions of 'direct' is to have re-established the fundamental importance of sound in film, an importance passed over in silence since the thirties. The 'lived word' (*parole*) recorded by Pierre Perrault, even if it is inserted in a naturalist system, still swept out stereotyped sound which had reigned in film previously.

In other respects, this technique imposed a redefinition of cinematographic fiction in that it makes evident its own process of representation and the process at work in all the successive operations of producing a film from the shooting script to mixing. In 'direct', fiction no longer pre-exists before the shooting but is truly its *product*. Inversely, a thought out use of direct underlines the element of obligatory manipulation in each and every cinematographic operation. It is true that, when practiced 'innocently', this technique is programmed by the most spontaneous ideology. But when used dialectically, inserted in a process which in the final analysis can only be fictional—even if we are dealing with a raw document—it lets us underline the split between reality and representative process and thus lets us put the accent on the materiality of the figurative operation at work in the shooting of a film.

The most productive aspects of direct manifest themselves in their consequences in fiction film, opening up another conception of the cinematographic 'subject' with films as different as *L'Amour fou* by Jacques Rivette, *The Moral Tales* by Eric Rohmer, *The Mother and the Whore* by Eustache and Jean Luc Godard's entire oeuvre from *Breathless* (1959) to *Numéro deux* (1975). Direct is really a manifestation of a new modality of voice recording in film.

THE PRODUCTION OF CINEMATIC REALITY

Mick Eaton

I—Technology and ideology

It would be possible—indeed it would be conventional—to provide an account of Rouch which would see his work as a progression, in conjunction with certain technological developments, towards an increasingly unmediated relationship to the reality of the pro-filmic event. The narrative of this tale of relentless technological progress towards the ultimate goal of an effacement of technology would commence with the early ethnographic shorts, inadequately realised on equipment allowing for 20 second shots, with no possibility of sync-sound, but already using a light 16mm camera without a tripod; then there would be the experiments with voice-over commentary (such as *Moi, un noir*) superseded by the invention of the light sync-sound camera which was able to capture directly people talking as they move through the world (*Chronique d'un été*, etc.); this would be followed by the experiments with sequence-length shots achieved 'on location' (such as *Gare du Nord*) leading on to the anthropological documentaries of the late sixties and the seventies in which all sound is recorded synchronous with the shooting of the images and most of the editing is done in the camera at the time of filming (*Tourou et Bitti*, etc.). The future would hold possibilities of even greater liberation from the constraints attendant on the need to use a 'recording technology' and further progression towards Truth captured 'directly' as cameras are developed with half-hour long magazines and with the person who operates the camera simultaneously recording the sound. As Rouch himself put it in a recent interview: 'Maybe in some years there will be a truly one-man system. A film maker will be able to work in the field by himself over a long period of time. He may have a small two-track Nagra tape-recorder, a microphone on the camera and possibly another omni-directional microphone. He'll have an earphone to monitor the sound as he's filming. The sound will be married later on. This will be the new race of film makers.'[1] Elsewhere, Rouch refers to this new age as the final realisation of Astruc's notion of the camera-stylo (the camera-pen),[2] but this instrument will be more like a cheap, readily available, 'democratic' Bic ball-point, rather than an expensive Parker.

This view, all too common in critical discourses accompanying direct cinema and ethnographic film practices, admits a necessary tension between the implicit assumption that the camera is a neutral recording device, and the explicit belief that the camera does actually intrude on the pro-filmic event, but it sees this tension as being resolved by recourse to technical

40

strategies which, eventually and hopefully, will be surmounted by means of the development of an increasingly unobtrusive technology. Until that day dawns it is necessary for the camera-operator to make him or herself unobtrusive, to blend into the setting, usually by getting to know the people being filmed well enough in advance of shooting.[3] The implication of this scenario for a film making practice might be phrased as follows: in the interaction of one reality (the physical presence of the camera) with another (the pro-filmic event) the adoption of a series of technical strategies (depending on what equipment is available at any particular time) is required to ensure a transparency of form through which content can travel unhindered, in order to communicate directly with an audience. Whilst this is the problematic in which the bulk of the writing on ethnographic film is contained, it can in no way be seen to contain Rouch's film practice without doing violence to the widely divergent types of film with which he has been associated throughout his career. Nevertheless, this is a position from which Rouch speaks (often) and to which he addresses himself (usually). A recognition of this problematic and of its implications is necessary if we are to understand Rouch's work as well as his often contradictory statements about it.

Whenever the camera is seen as a device which can, under the right circumstances, record reality directly, there must always be, by necessity, a recourse to two opposing concepts which, whilst they cannot be termed theoretical, are profoundly ideological, and which plague most of the writing on Rouch's work. These are, on the one hand, a technological determinism, and, on the other, notions of the 'natural language' of the cinema.[4] Technological determinism argues that a film is only as adequate to the reality of the pro-filmic event as its technology allows it to be, implying the absurd corollary that with every technical development the film practice of the past is rendered obsolete, further from the real. Documentary films of the past are able to be recuperated only as pieces of history, as 'fore-runners' of contemporary practice—fore-warned but not fore-armed. This argument is wheeled in by writers on documentary film to remove any examination of either ideology or aesthetics. Cinema technology and its effects, mobilised at the time of shooting, and grounded in an all-encompassing liberal world-view (which is able to re-write ideology as the 'point-of-view' of the film maker[5]) become the site of the production of meaning. As Louis Marcorelles says[6] of 16 mm, it is 'not so much a technique as a state of mind, the natural breathing of an art that has been revived through contact with the real world.' We remember how Comolli and Narboni described direct cinema: 'That magical notion of "seeing is believing": ideology goes on display to prevent itself from being shown up for what it really is, contemplates itself but does not criticise itself.'[7]

Aesthetics are removed as evidence of the 'beautiful', which must obviously indicate a fictional mediation: if direct cinema films are beautiful then this can only mean that reality is itself beautiful, since the aesthetic filter has been removed and we are asked to accept that these films are not 'art'

41

but 'life'. Two statements by Rouch from different periods in his life can serve to illustrate this point. Firstly: 'The beautiful shot is the worst trap one can fall into in the cinema. Leacock believes that a bad, unlovely shot is a guarantee of authenticity. It's direct cinema: one follows, one reports an event. The aesthetic quality of the visuals is secondary, of little importance.'[8] And secondly: 'I've always been wary of beautiful photography. It means there's nothing in it. The beauty is in the core which comes out: all of a sudden an emotion emerges and it's completely unexpected. I stay away from *la belle image* [*lovely images*]. Aestheticism is the great danger.'[9]

The notion of the natural language of the cinema is one of the ways cinema has thought itself since its first flickerings in the days of Lumière. More recently, we think of Bazin's statements regarding cinema's ontological realism and of Pasolini's semiotics of the real, in which cinema is granted the status of a language, but only that of a natural language which 'expresses reality not through symbols but via reality itself. If I want to express that tree I express it through itself. The cinema is a language that expresses reality with reality'.[10] Of course what is being repressed here is the work of signification—the necessity to see film as a specific signifying practice in which meaning is produced by the articulation of heterogeneous signifying elements—a repression whose aim is the preservation of the homogeneous nature of reality which can be easily and unproblematically rendered visible. Significantly, both of the above mentioned attempts to theorise cinema's role in terms of the duplication of 'reality' required the validation of certain technical strategies. For Bazin this meant emphasising the long take, deep focus, etc., for Pasolini, the use of non-professional actors, real locations, and so on. So with Rouch, we are asked to see a number of identifiable 'Rouchian traits', such as the ten minute sequence shot, the use of hand-held camera, the avoidance of the zoom, the sync-sound overlaid with (often) personal commentary, etc., as an inventory of techniques (states of mind?) or strategies that are almost inevitable, given present technology, if one is to render visible what is already observable, rather than considering these as evidence of semiotic activity, structuring the text and providing points of entry for the spectator. For the films of Rouch are presented to us not as texts, but as evidences (and we remember Bazin's famous comparison of the cinema with the shroud of Turin). Again, it is worth mentioning at this point that in the discourses surrounding direct cinema, as in Bazin's aesthetic, editing (montage) is cast as the villain in cinema's quest for the holy grail—regarded as a distortion, a formalist cul-de-sac, and that these ideas have fed naturally into Rouch's practice. However, in a film such as *Gare du Nord*, which in its welding together of two ten minute takes effaces montage altogether and fuses real time and film time, all the movements of the camera are predicated on the construction of a coherent cinematic space. The movements of the camera follow quite closely a conventional 'classic realist' account of the action with the creation of a point of identification between the eye of the camera and the eye of the spectator, and nothing in the film seems to suggest that such a position, rather than the montage classically deployed to create it, is itself a problem. In this context it would be illuminating to compare *Gare du Nord* with a film such as *Condition of Illusion* by Peter Gidal, which uses the hand-held 16 mm camera precisely to deny the production of a coherent cinematic space.

So in a situation where notions of technological determinism and natural language will be mobilised to ensure the defence of the image as ideologically neutral, it becomes increasingly important, before we can approach Rouch's films as texts, to contextualise his work particularly in relation to institutional validations of 'ethnographic film', to questions of audience and spectator–text relationships, and in relation to the 'truth' of cinema vérité. Not that this contextualisation should in any way be used to 'explain' a practice, nor even that it could do so. But rather that it may provide bases from which to interrogate the discourses surrounding direct cinema (including those writings and fragments of interviews by Rouch reproduced here in which he talks of his own work and that of others), to interrogate these discourses and to tease out the contradictions they present, in order to provide a prologue to a study of documentary films which would be operating from within semiotics and to free the reception of the films of Rouch from a framework in which they are to be considered as reflections of a pre-given and unproblematically determined reality. This endeavour is not undertaken to provide an alternative to available discourses on the 'social role' of documentary, but rather to stand in fundamental opposition to those discourses which are at the disposal of those who have so much invested in a world which can be easily rendered visible and available for our gaze—discourses which so often go unchallenged and which are used continually to silence the voices which do not echo theirs.

II—Anthropology and audience

I have argued elsewhere[11] that the metalanguage that enables the spectators of ethnographic film to advance towards knowledge (knowledge posed as an uncovering, a revelation of the rationality of the 'real' pro-filmic event and its participants) and which attempts to contain and bind the heterogeneous discourses of the film text into a homogeneous unity is not the narrative, as cine-semioticians have argued in relation to classic realist cinema, but an anthropological discourse. The discourse of anthropology (constituted as a discipline in a specific institutional formation), whether it be supplied by the commentary or by the institutional framework of the exhibition and distribution of ethnographic films, provides the point of origin of these films—specifying them as, precisely, 'ethnographic'. To this end the marks of meaning production in ethnographic films need to be effaced so that they can be used as part of a pedagogic practice, where they provide 'surrogate field-work experience' for the student of anthropology as well as a 'record' of techniques and practices which may well disappear in the future. Broadly speaking, this produces ethnographic film as the cinematic practice which is the polar opposite of 'art cinema' or of those tendencies within the avant-garde where the 'view of reality' constructed in the film is offered as readable by recourse to the biography of the film maker as 'artist' or 'visionary', constructed outside the film text (we might think here of the films of Stan Brakhage, for example, available as 'documentaries' of the artist's refined sense of perception, or, perhaps more pertinently in this context, Peter Kubelka's *Unsere Afrikareise*, offered as the artist's synthesis and distillation of the experience of a trip to Africa).

I would argue that this general characterisation of ethnographic film is not applicable to the heterogeneous range of film practices associated with Rouch throughout the thirty years he has been involved in film making, even though the bulk of his films are short examinations of 'events' such as a particular technique or a particular ritual practice, whose exhibition is, I would imagine, almost exclusively confined to pedagogical presentations within and around the Musée de l'Homme, the French equivalent of the Museum of Mankind. So Rouch's (impossible) task becomes to free his work from the constraints imposed by the needs of the institutional discourse, to refuse to offer his films as transparent evidences for the positivism of the anthropological encounter, whilst at the same time remaining within the terms of the discourse of anthropology, remaining as a central figure in debates surrounding ethnographic film. Indeed, in his position as compiler of UNESCO catalogues of ethnographic films and as judge in international festivals, he is situated as an arbiter and historian of that practice. How he attempts to resolve these contradictions can be seen in the extracts published in this book from *The Camera and Man*.

Because of the total conflation of technology and aesthetics, the history of ethnographic film is seen as a dialectic between 'the camera' and 'man'—with the highest achievements being realised when the two terms are united: for example, when Rouch the film maker is his own camera-man. In this way, there is a constant inscription of the personal into the pedagogical, not only in such films as *Chronique d'un été* (where we see and hear Rouch, captured by other camera-men) but, more significantly, in films such as *Tourou et Bitti*, where Rouch's presence as camera-man is seen to alter the terms of the pro-filmic event and where this presence becomes part of the 'truth' that the camera records. So the technological possibilities for self effacement offered to the ethnographic film maker are systematically refused by Rouch in the inscription of the personal and the subjective into the body of the film text.

To pursue this argument further it is necessary to interrogate the answers Rouch gives to the question: 'For whom do you make your films?' Firstly, he replies, 'For me.' Rouch thus becomes the ultimate guarantor, not so much of the truth of the event being filmed or the authenticity of the camera's relationship to it, but more the guarantor of the knowledge, an almost mystical knowledge, of the necessity that this particular event, rather than any other, should be shot. Any audience the films construct must, it would seem, be complicit in taking on trust that Rouch knows what to film and when to film it. Incidentally, because Rouch is thus posed as 'the first viewer' (through the viewfinder of his camera) and the 'first editor' (by deciding when to pull the trigger on his camera) of his films, his relationship to editors, when he uses them, becomes very specific. For Rouch the editor is not someone whose job is to construct coherence from the mass of raw footage he has shot. That has been achieved already by Rouch himself, editing in the camera as he shoots. Rather, the editor, the 'second viewer', is a technician, an outsider to the pro-filmic event, who can tell Rouch whether or not he is communicating effectively. That is to say, the editor is not at all supposed to be implicated in the process of meaning production. This not only serves to indicate that the moment of production is privileged in this practice over all other instances (including the moment of consumption). But also, more crucially it points us to the necessity to examine Rouch's relationships with 'technicians' in order to deny the terms of the argument presented, as we have already seen, so often in relation to documentary film practice, i.e. that technology is the determining factor on the presentation of the pro-filmic event. In this context it is necessary only to mention Rouch's involvement with the production of the K.M.T. camera at Eclair, as well as his recent interest in and involvement with Beauviala's experiments to produce a single-system 16mm camera at Aäton.[12] It thus becomes increasingly untenable to maintain that technological developments are outside of historical and ideological determination.[13]

The second answer Rouch gives to the question for whom he makes his films is, for him, undoubtedly the most important: after himself, the films are made for the people who participated in the pro-filmic event. This has been a constant element in Rouch's film making practice since the earliest days and its mythical charter derives from the stories of Flaherty developing the rushes of *Nanook* in his igloo in order to show them to the Eskimos. Because of this the camera and man are fused even more directly—the camera takes on specifically human attributes, it becomes 'the participant camera'. Added to this, the project of anthropology is transformed. It becomes 'shared anthropology', accounting for a film such as *Petit à Petit*, which brings the anthropological encounter back to Paris, removing the stain of colonialism from the practice of ethnographic field-work and opening the possibility of a 'dialogue' between cultures. The insistence on the involvement of the participants as audience of the film (literally represented in the penultimate sequence of *Chronique d'un été* where the reactions of the participants who have just seen the rushes is filmed and becomes part of the final film) is justified by recourse to two arguments: one might be termed the 'personal humanist' argument, the other the 'universal scientific' argument. The first is 'to show another how I see him', to demonstrate, for example, to the African villager what it is that Rouch has been doing in his village all this time, to convince the native that he is not a colonial administrator, or that he has not been making Tarzan movies. This allows for a validation of visual anthropology which, far from being subservient to the demands of anthropology as a discipline, actually grants it a superior status, as the ethnographic monograph, contrary to film, rarely if ever finds its way back

45

to the village to be read by informants. This argument again implicitly calls on the idea that film presents a natural language which can be read by anybody. Secondly, though, the necessity of screening the film to the participants in the pro-filmic event is defended on the grounds that the film can be viewed with informants in order to arrive, quickly and easily, at material for ethnographic consideration. So, anthropology's demands are satisfied and superseded at the same time: film is a research tool for the anthropologist, but one which is more efficient than the others. Two extracts from a recent interview with Rouch illustrate this point: 'Take this film about hippopotamus hunting . . . I showed this film to the hippopotamus hunters themselves two years after it was shot. I went to their village with a generator. Maybe only 10% of them had seen a film before. We put the screen on the wall of a house. When we started they all gathered around the projector. They thought something would happen there. Then they suddenly discovered that something was happening on the screen. But after only one minute they were *in* the film, there were no problems. They understood it.' 'With the use of light equipment, synchronised sound film, long sequence shots, it is clear that you can do more with film than you can by means of direct observation. Indirect observation is more and more important because you can work on the film with the people who are actually in it. You can make a study of the ritual with the priest. It's impossible to stop a priest in the middle of a mass to say "why are you going from the right side of the altar to the left?" But with a film you can do that. You can discuss it afterwards. You can get more and more feedback from the participants.'[14]

However, it is the third answer Rouch gives regarding the intended audience which poses real difficulties for considerations of exhibition and distribution, let alone spectator-text relationships. Again Rouch strives for a happy synthesis of the personal and the pedagogical, but this is not easily achieved as becomes evident in his final reply to the question as to who these films are for: 'For the greatest number of people, for everyone.' In the 1955 article on ethnographic films in *Positif*, Rouch had argued for the necessity of these films to be seen by a large audience in the interests of humanism and global understanding, so that all people will realise, through the medium of film, that people all over the world are just like themselves: 'As for those who know nothing of ethnography they will discover that other men are not the "savages" of fable and that their social institutions are just as complicated as ours, their religions just as worthy of respect, their behaviour just as logical. They will discover above all that films can be made which are just as exciting as all the Tarzan movies in the world simply by filming what is there, and not what one wishes were there.'[15]

Similarly, he argues in *The Camera and Man*[16] that if these films do not obtain a wide distribution, the fault may well be with the films themselves. That is to say, that his films should not so much serve the interests of anthropology as a discipline constructed outside of cinema, but rather that they should serve the interests of universal human understanding. He says, though I cannot claim in any way to understand what he means, that 'it is time for ethnographic films to become films in their own right'. This seems to be in direct contradiction with something he says earlier on in the same paper: a contradiction which once more takes us back to the central notion of the natural language of direct cinema, in this instance seen in opposition to the commercialism and artifice of, say, Hollywood cinema (a convenient shorthand for the industrial site of the production of such films as *Sanders of the River, Tarzan*, etc.). Rouch says: 'When universities, cultural institutes, and television stations can show these films without having to make them conform to commercial productions, but rather can accept their differences, a new type of ethnographic film with its own specific criteria may be developed.'[17] In other words, the standards of 'commercial production' not only block the exhibition and distribution of ethnographic films, but they also prevent these films from developing as, presumably, 'cinema in their own right.'

In simplified terms, the irresolvable contradiction inherent in Rouch's presentation of his film practice resides between the humanist ideology to which he appeals and the constraints imposed by the institutionalised discourses of ethnography which function as the encompassing metalanguage 'placing' the films. This metalanguage requires the total effacement of the marks of meaning production which are considered, at worst, to be 'artifice', or, at best, unfortunate technological imperfections or limitations. The metalanguage also demands that the viewer be positioned as the observer of the unfolding of the visible, the recipient of information/ revelation and in no way responsible for or implicated in the production of meaning. The demands of a humanism grounded in assumptions about a transcendental essence of humanity and denying the specificity of differences in favour of a notion of universal communication and recognition, call for a wide distribution of the films and for mass audiences. If the films fail to secure these things, then this must be due to the films as much as if not more than to the practices and institutions governing distribution and exhibition. However, at the same time, the need to conform to the demands of the defining metalanguage confines the films, regardless of their success or failure on the humanist level, almost exclusively to specialised exhibition and distribution circuits: the non-entertainment sector as embodied in cultural/educational institutions and their equivalent places in the television apparatus.[18]

How does Rouch attempt to resolve this contradiction? Sometimes simply by pretending that it does not exist, claiming that his films are not in conflict with the project of anthropology, and that the difference is merely that they are inherently more dramatic: '"Good anthropology" is not a wide description of everything, but a close identification of one technique or ritual. The rituals are supposed to be dramatic. They are creations of the people who want them to be interesting and exciting . . . What you can't get in writing is the drama of the ritual. Writing can't have that effect. That's the whole point of visual anthropology.'[19] It is their drama and excitement which makes the films unproblematically available to a large audience: 'Between filming men and observing them there is, when it comes down to it, only a small difference in methods: the initial preparation and the preliminary enquiry, shooting and observation, editing and the final writing up are the three essential stages of the work of the cineaste and the ethnographer. Simply, the cineaste writes with a camera on film stock, and the ethnographer writes with a biro on a note pad. Then the former puts together on an editing table what the latter puts together on a typewriter. It's only later that a big difference can be seen: all films, even bad ones, are seen by a large public, whilst ethnographic monographs and articles, even excellent ones, are never read by anyone.'[20]

More interestingly, in terms of Rouch's undoubted though often unacknowledged influence on New Wave film makers as well as in terms of his possible influence on a younger generation of Anglo-American documentary film makers for whom the bulk of his work may well remain unknown, Rouch frequently attempts to resolve this contradiction by means of a tried and tested strategy which consists simply of the production of an author, the inscription of Rouch himself, the film maker/cameraman, into the work. In this way, an attempt is made to produce an authorial instance for the films which will, hopefully, hold the contradictions within this third term which articulates the 'real' and its representation. On the one hand, the figure of the ethnographer guarantees the authenticity of the observation, while on the other hand, according to conventional humanist notions of artistic production, it also functions to signal that it is a matter of one human being communicating with others. It is through the detour of the figure of the author that the audience can thus recognise its own 'humanity' in the 'people' (re)presented in/by the film. This inscription, to be read across the semiotics of the text, is present in every aspect of Rouch's work, from the way he films (for the most part the crew consists only of himself and a few trusted African soundmen), through the way the commentaries are overlaid onto the image-track, to the way in which Rouch himself is so often present at the screenings of his films at festivals, anthropological conventions and his saturday seminars in Paris.

Although Rouch defends his way of working alone by referring to the necessity not to disturb the pro-filmic event,[21] it is clear that this is not his prime concern, nor has he ever espoused any of the more naive formulations of this argument.[22] His call for a participatory cinema is clearly based on assumptions that ethnographic enquiry can never be objective: 'Most people refuse to recognise that any anthropology must destroy what it investigates. Even if you are making a long distance observation of breast feeding you disturb the mother and her infant, even if you don't think so. The fundamental problem in all social sciences is that the facts are always distorted by the presence of the person who asks the questions. You distort the answer simply by asking the question.'[23] The way out for Rouch is to inscribe himself (as observer) as one of the participants in the scene we are witnessing, as one of the stars of the spectacle offered to us. So we are not asked to be the observers of an event, a ritual, a dance, etc. but rather the *observers of an observation of an event.*

In relation to this we might consider the commentaries to Rouch's films, for it is here that he situates himself furthest from the concerns of contemporary ethnographic film making. With the development of light sync-sound cameras the practice of subtitling the words of informants has become almost mandatory in Anglo-American ethnographic film circles,[24] defended as a way of allowing the people filmed to 'speak for themselves'. But Rouch has vehemently resisted this practice, preferring to use a certain kind of voice-over commentary which he has used ever since his earliest films when sync-sound was not available. Of this Rouch says: 'I believe the image is of paramount importance. Subtitles destroy the image. I want to look at the film; I have to see it twice—the first time to understand what's cooking and the second time to look at the image ... it's a sacrilege to destroy an image with subtitles.'[25]

However, the way he uses voice-over rather than preserving the primacy of the image sets up a completely different relationship between sound and image than that present in either the institutionally validated documentary film (where informants' speech is captured directly and commentary used either to describe the images or to provide an anthropological interpretation) or in the classic commercial spectacle (where each 'character' speaks his/her fiction). We think of the 'sociology' of the commentary of *Les maîtres fous* (for the English version of which Rouch preferred to speak himself, in his own 'bad English' rather than let someone else read a translation of his words written and spoken in French), of the 'poetry' of the commentary of *La chasse au lion à l'arc* (where our memories, distilled from a thousand Tarzan movies, of 'Africa, the dark continent' find a presence in the repeated phrases 'the mountains of crystal, the mountains of the moon.'), and of the 'incantations' of the commentary of *Les funérailles du vieil Anaï* (where Rouch does not merely translate the Dogon funeral incantation for us, but rather acts it out, taking on the role of the priest, whilst at the same time we see the 'real' priest and hear his synchronous incantation under that of Rouch). We might also think of the picaresque commentaries of the African participants of *Moi, un noir* and *Jaguar*, telling their tales long after the films were shot and slipping from the first to the third person, from the past to the present tense when talking of themselves. Peter Wollen has suggested[26] that it is Rouch's use of the voice-over commentary that has been his major influence on the work of Godard, and it is this which situates his work as radically eccentric to the concerns of ethnographic film making. But for Rouch himself the commentary provides the means whereby he can insert himself into the finished film and his remarks about preserving the primacy of the image are predicated on the fact that Rouch himself is the guarantor of the necessity of that image being there in the first place, that his eye is not only filming for us, but is presented to us as an essential part of the filmed spectacle: 'Objectivity consists in inserting what one knows into what one films, inserting oneself with a tool which will provoke the emergence of a certain reality . . . When I have a camera and a microphone I'm not my usual self, I'm in a strange state, in a *cine-transe*. This is the objectivity one can expect, being perfectly conscious that the camera is there and that people know it. From that moment we live in an audio-visual galaxy; a new truth emerges, cinema vérité, which has nothing to do with normal reality.'[27]

The inscription of self into the film is defined mystically, in the concept of the *cine-transe*, but, at the same time, because Rouch is an anthropologist and the mystical is always amenable to anthropological investigation, it is defined scientifically, objectively: cinema vérité. Going on from this it becomes possible to say that the inscription of the author into the text resolves the contradiction between anthropology and audience (to put it crudely) by re-defining anthropology as 'essentially subjective', indeed 'poetic'. It is this notion which underlies many of Rouch's explicitly fictional films. We think, for example, of his references to surrealism in relation to *La punition, Gare du Nord*, and *Petit à Petit*. But it is a surrealism conveyed by the theme of the encounter, an encounter to be seen as acting metaphorically on the project of anthropology. If the human sciences are to be seen as essentially poetic then the presence of an author will continually fall on the film stock: 'I consider myself a film maker as well as an ethnographer, I believe that ethnography is poetry. I don't really believe in the human sciences very much, I've said so many times. The human sciences have something terribly subjective about them in the last analysis. The films are in spite of everything *auteur* films, by their method and by their point of view. I know another film maker or cameraman wouldn't do it the same way.'[28]

III—Truth, transe and provocation

What, then, is the basis of this objectivity, this 'cinema-truth' which Rouch talks of as being nothing to do with normal reality? Why is it that in an interview conducted towards the end of 1977 he persists in using a term such as cinema vérité which had been conveniently dropped, as an embarrassment, by documentary film makers in favour of the term direct cinema, suggested by Mario Ruspoli at the Marché International des Programmes et Equipements de Télévision at Lyons in 1963? The term cinema vérité is thought to have derived from the article by Edgar Morin, *Pour un nouveau cinéma vérité*,[29] a report on the international festival of ethnographic film in Florence, where he had been a member of the jury together with Rouch. Though Morin's term was designed to be an explicit reference and tribute to Dziga Vertov's notion of Kino-Pravda, it is clear that for Morin the emphasis in the phrase was, as Marsolais points out, on the newness, rather than on the 'cinema vérité'. For Morin adds that the father of this type of practice is 'more Flaherty than Dziga Vertov' and whenever in subsequent years Rouch makes reference to the strange bedfellows who apparently conceived the bastard cinema vérité, there is always an uneasy relationship to Vertov, presumably because of his experiments with montage and his relationship to formalism. What Rouch wishes to recuperate from Vertov is not the notion of the cinema-eye, radically different from the human eye, but rather the possibility of a marriage, a synthesis, between the human eye and the cinema-eye—a fusion whose result will be a greater humanity and a greater objectivity at the same time.

When the film on which Rouch and Morin collaborated, *Chronique d'un été*, was released, it bore the subtitle 'an experiment in cinema vérité'. But for Rouch this was never meant to indicate that he claimed to be capturing reality directly, without fictional mediation. This practice was not reducible to the 'photo journalism' of Leacock, Pennebaker and the Maysles' notion of 'living cinema', for example, in which the director/cameraman films in a situation of crisis so acute that the effect of his presence is deemed to be minimal (as in *The Chair*) or in a public situation where many other journalists and outsiders are present but where the camera can capture the 'private' aspect of the 'public' event (as in *Primary*). Rouch defended his film practice in a very different way. As noted earlier, he emphasises his presence as a crucial factor. Crucial not so much because the people who know him and trust him can reveal themselves openly, honestly and directly to us through the medium of Rouch and his camera, but because in the disjunction caused by the very presence of the camera, people will act, will lie, will be uncomfortable, and it is the manifestation of this side of themselves which is regarded as a more profound revelation than anything a 'candid camera' or 'living cinema' ever could reveal: 'There is a whole series of intermediaries, and these are lying intermediaries. We contract time, we extend it, we choose an angle for the shot, we deform the people we're shooting, we speed things up and follow one movement to the detriment of another movement. So there is a whole work of lies. But, for me and Edgar Morin at the time we made that film this lie was more real than the truth. That is to say, there was a certain number of things happening, human facts surrounding us . . . which people would not have been able to say any other way . . . It's a sort of catalyst which allows us to reveal, with doubts, a fictional part of all of us, but which for me is the most real part of an individual.'[30]

The camera, fused with the presence of its operator, is a catalyst, an accelerator, conceived of as an absolutely necessary presence, not to be hidden or minimised, but foregrounded, inscribed into the film text: 'Very quickly I discovered the camera was something else: it was not a brake but let's say, to use an automobile term, an accelerator. You push these people to confess themselves and it seemed to us without any limit. Some of the public who saw the film [*Chronicle*] said the film was a film of exhibitionists. I don't think so. It's not exactly exhibitionism: it's a very strange kind of confession in front of the camera, where the camera is, let's say, a mirror, and also a window open to the outside.'[31]

Rouch conceives of cinema vérité as cinema-provocation: 'Not to film life as it is, but life as it is provoked'.[32] And from this act of provocation a different kind of cinema emerges, conceived of as neither documentary truth,

51

for the participants are always performing, taking on roles, nor theatrical fiction, for the role they adopt is conceived of as more real than the real. A cinema in which Rouch plays the shaman, the master of ceremonies at a cinematic ritual, stimulating and entering the transe with his camera as the magician's instrument wielded so that a new truth can be revealed which is not the 'truth' of the pro-filmic event, but the 'truth' of cinema itself—'cinema is the creation of a new reality'.[33]

All this is necessary to situate Rouch, as Fieschi maintains in the essay reprinted here, firmly in the realm of fiction, but at the same time to specify the conditions of the production of that fiction. In other words, the relationship of the spectator to the text is always, necessarily, a fictional relationship. As Metz says: 'Every film is a fictional film'. 'Characteristic of the cinema is not the imaginary that it may happen to represent, it is the imaginary that it *is* from the start, the imaginary that constitutes it as a signifier . . . In the cinema it is not just the fictional signified, if there is one, that is present in the mode of absence, it is from the outset the signifier.'[34] Any 'reality' that the cinema of Rouch points us towards will not be reality amenable to pedagogical explanation within the discourse of anthropology, but will be a reality specific to the cinematic representation and the space allowed for us as spectators of that representation, attending to it and held, 'entertained' in/by its processes of signification.

NOTES

1 Interview with Jean Rouch by James Potts in *Educational Broadcasting International*, vol. 11, no. 2, June 1978.
2 Alexandre Astruc's term 'camera stylo' was first used in his article *The Birth of a New Avant Garde: the Camera Stylo*, in *Ecran Français*, no. 144, 1948, reprinted in English in *The New Wave*, Peter Graham (ed.), Cinema One, London 1968. For Rouch's extension of the metaphor, see *Aux Sources du Cinéma-Vérité avec Jean Rouch*, interview with Rouch by Raymond Bellour and Maurice Frydland in *Cinema 63*, no. 72, January 1963.
3 For a development of this problematic, see, for example, *Living Cinema* by Louis Marcorelles, London, George Allen and Unwin, 1973 and *Cinéma Vérité* by M. Ali Issari, as well as many papers in *Principles of Visual Anthropology*, Paul Hockings (ed), Mouton, the Hague 1975. For a useful inventory of guidelines for making ethnographic films, see *The Needs of Ethnographic Films* by Jerry W. Leach in *Cambridge Anthropology, Special issue on Ethnographic Film*, 1977.
4 See *The Camera I—Observations on Documentary* by Annette Kuhn in *Screen*, vol. 19, no. 2, Summer 1978.
5 For an interesting discussion of this area, see *Triumph of the Will—Notes on Documentary and Spectacle* by Steve Neale, in *Screen*, vol. 20, no. 1, spring 1979.
6 Marcorelles, *op. cit.*
7 *Cinema/Ideology/Criticism* by Jean-Louis Comolli and Jean Narboni in *Screen Reader 1*, 1977.
8 Interview with Rouch by Ian Cameron and Mark Shivas in *Movie*, no. 8, April 1963.
9 *Cine-Transe—the Vision of Jean Rouch*, interview by Dan Yakir in *Film Quarterly*, vol. 31, no. 3, spring 1978.
10 *Pasolini on Pasolini*, Oswald Stack (ed.), Cinema One, London 1969.
11 *Film and Anthropology* by M. Eaton and I. Ward in *Screen*, vol. 17, no. 3, autumn 1976.

12 See the long interview with Jean-Pierre Beauviala in *Cahiers du Cinéma*, nos 285–288, February–May 1978. Incidentally, Rouch has talked of a plan to make a film with Beauviala in the role of Dionysus.

13 Annette Kuhn, *op. cit.*

14 Both these quotations from the E.B.I. interview, *op. cit.*

15 *A Propos des Films Ethnographiques* by Jean Rouch in *Positif*, nos 14/15, 1955 (trans. M.E.).

16 In *Principles of Visual Anthropology*, *op. cit.* Page 62 in this monograph.

17 *Ibid.*

18 For a discussion of some of the conditions bearing on an ethnographic film made for television see *Some Women of Marrakech* by Liz Brown in *Screen*, vol. 19, no. 2, summer 1978.

19 *The Politics of Visual Anthropology*, an interview with Rouch by Dan Georgeakas, Udayan Gupta and Judy Janda in *Cineaste*, vol. 8, no. 4, summer 1978.

20 *Positif, op. cit.*

21 *The camera and Man*, p. 55 in this monograph.

22 See, for example, Margaret Mead: 'The camera that stays in one spot, that is not turned, wound, refocused or visibly loaded does become part of the background scene—what it records did happen.' in *Visual Anthropology in a Discipline of Words* in Hockings (ed.) *op. cit.*

23 *Cineaste* interview, *op. cit.*

24 See films such as *To Live with Herds* by David and Judith MacDougall; *Trobriand Cricket* by Gary Kildea and Jerry Leach, as well as many of the later films in Granada Television's *Disappearing World* series.

25 E.B.I. interview, *op. cit.*

26 Personal communication.

27 *Film Quarterly* interview, *op. cit.*

28 Interview with Rouch in *Le Monde*, 16 June, 1971.

29 In *France-Observateur*, no. 506, 14 January, 1960.

30 *Jean Rouch—Les aventures d'un nègre blanc*, interview with Rouch by Philippe Esnault in *Image et Son*, no. 249, April 1971.

31 *Movie* interview, *op. cit.*

32 *Ibid.*

33 *Ibid.*

34 *The Imaginary Signifier* by Christian Metz in *Screen*, vol. 16, no. 2, summer 1975.

The Camera and Man

(*Extract*)

Jean Rouch

Ethnographic cinema today

Today, we have quite extraordinary equipment available and, ever since 1960, the number and the quality of the ethnographic films produced throughout the world has increased yearly (more than seventy films were submitted to the selection committee for the first Venezia Genti in 1971). However, ethnographic film, in spite of its marginal and yet quite specific aspects, has really not yet found its proper path. After having resolved all the technical problems, we must seemingly re-invent, like Flaherty or Vertov in the 1920's, the rules of a new language which might allow us to cross the boundaries between all civilizations.

It is not my concern here to evaluate all of the experiments and trends in the field of ethnographic film, but rather to reveal those which seem to me to be the most pertinent.

Ethnographic film and commercial cinema

Although there are no technical factors preventing it, wide distribution of ethnographic films is extremely rare. However, the majority of ethnographic films produced within the last few years have ALWAYS been made with the techniques of commercial cinema: credits, original music, sophisticated editing, commentary for the masses, appropriate length, etc. . . .

Most of the time, then, what results is a hybrid product satisfying neither scientific rigors nor film aesthetics. Of course, some masterpieces or original works escape from this inevitable trap. Ethnographers consider film to be like a book, and a book on ethnology appears no different from an ordinary book.

The result is a notorious rise in the prime cost of these films. This makes the almost total absence of commercial distribution even more harshly felt, especially when the market for films remains so open to sensational documentaries like *Mondo Cane*.

Obviously, there will always be exceptions: *The Hadza* made by the young film maker Sean Hudson in close collaboration with the anthropologist James Woodburn, or *Emu Ritual at Ruguri* and the whole Australian series of the producer-film maker Roger Sandall in collaboration with an anthropologist again, or *The Feast* in which Timothy Asch immersed himself completely in the research of Napoleon Chagnon among the Yąnomamö.

The solution to this problem is the study of the distribution network of these films. When universities, cultural institutes, and television stations can show these films without having to make them conform to commercial productions but rather can accept their differences, a new type of ethnographic film with its own specific criteria may be developed.

Ethnographer-film maker or team of film maker-plus-ethnographer?

It is for similar reasons, to 'take advantage of all technical skills available,' that ethnologists over the past few years have preferred not to do the filming themselves but instead to call upon a team of technicians for the job (actually, it is the technical crew—sent out by a television production unit—who call upon the ethnologist).

Personally—unless forced into a special situation—I am violently opposed to film crews. My reasons are several. The sound engineer must fully understand the language of the people he is recording. It is thus indispensable that he belong to the ethnic group being filmed and that he also be trained in the minutiae of his job. Besides, with the present techniques used in direct cinema (synchronic sound), the film maker must be the cameraman. And the ethnologist alone, in my mind, is the one who knows when, where, and how to film, i.e. to do the production. Finally, and this is doubtless the decisive argument, the ethnologist should spend quite a long time in the field before undertaking the least bit of film making. This period of reflection, of learning, of mutual understanding might be extremely long (Robert Flaherty spent a year in the Samoan Islands before shooting the first foot of film there), but such a stay is incompatible with the schedules and salaries of a team of technicians.

The films of Asen Balikci on the Netsilik Eskimo or the recent series of films by Ian Dunlop on the Baruya of New Guinea are for me good examples of what must not happen again. For these productions a superior crew of technicians intruded into a hostile land in spite of the presence of an anthropologist. Every time a film is shot, privacy is violated; but when the film maker-ethnologist is alone, when he cannot lean on his group of foreigners (two whites in an African village already form a community, a foreign body which is solid and thus risks rejection), the responsibility for any impurity can only be assumed by this one man. I have always wondered how that small group of Eskimos reacted to those crazy white men who made them clear their camp of good canned food.

This ambiguity probably did not appear in the *Desert People* series because the film makers and the aboriginal family they were filming spent time making their way through the desert together. But it is naturally apparent in the film on New Guinea, at the extraordinary end of the ceremony, when the group responsible for the initiation does not actually reject the film makers but asks their anthropologist friend if he can limit the distribution of the film. They asked that the film be seen only outside New Guinea (*a posteriori* rejection). At any rate, the complexity of the technical procedure was an obstacle to the 'participant camera.'

This is why it seems indispensable to me to initiate anthropology students into the techniques of recording both pictures and sound. Even if their films are technically quite inferior to the work of professionals, they will have the irreplaceable quality of real contact between the person filming and those being filmed.

Tripod camera or hand-held camea—zoom or fixed lens?

When American television networks were looking for films after World War II (particularly the *Adventure* series of Sol Lesser or of CBS), films shot without a tripod were almost unacceptable because of the consequent lack of stability. However, most of the war reporting done on 16mm film (e.g. the extraordinary *Memphis Bell*, actual adventures of a Fying Fortress filmed in 16mm and the first film to be enlarged to 35mm) had been done with hand-held cameras. But in fact, if some of us were to follow the example of these pioneers and film without a tripod, it was to economize and allow quick magazine changes between shots. The camera was stationary most of the time, panned sometimes and, on exceptional occasions, moved about ('crane' effect achieved by squatting, or traveling in a car).

It took the audacity of the young team from the National Film Board of Canada to free the camera from this impossibility. In 1954, *Corral* by Koenig and Kroitor pointed out a path later opened up more definitively in 1959 by what has become today's classic model of the traveling shot, i.e. when the camera follows the revolver of the bank guard in *Bientôt Noël*. When Michel Brault came to Paris to shoot *Chronique d'un été*, it was a revelation for all of us and for the television cameramen as well. The shot from *Primary* in which Leacock follows the entrance of John F. Kennedy was without a doubt the masterpiece of this new style of filming.

Since then camera designers have made considerable efforts to improve the manageability and balance of cine cameras. And today, all direct cinema cameramen know how to walk with their cameras, which have thus become the living cameras, the 'cine-eye' of Vertov.

In the area of ethnographic film, this technique seems to me to be particularly useful because it allows the cameraman to adapt himself to the action as a function of space, to generate reality rather than leave it simply to unfold before the viewer.

However, some producers continue to use tripods most of the time. This is probably done for technical reasons, and it is, to my mind, the major fault of the films of Roger Sandall and especially of the latest films of Ian Dunlop from New Guinea (it is not an accident that these are both Australian-based producers, since the best tripods and the best 'panoramic heads' are made in Sydney!) The immobility of the filming apparatus is compensated for by the extensive use of zoom lenses which give the optical effect of a dolly shot. In fact, these artificial techniques for simulating movement back and forth do not really succeed in letting one forget the rigidity of the camera which only sees from a SINGLE POINT OF VIEW. Despite the obviously intriguing nature of these casual ballets, we have to remember that the forward and backward movements are only optical and that the camera does not move closer to the subjects. The zoom lens is more like a voyeur who watches and notes details from atop a distant perch.

This involuntary arrogance of the camera is not only felt *a posteriori* by the attentive audience, but the subjects themselves perceive it even more strongly as an OBSERVATION POST.

For me, then, the only way to film is to walk about with the camera, taking it to wherever it is the most effective, and improvising a ballet in which the camera itself becomes just as much alive as the people it is filming. This would be the first synthesis between the theories of Vertov about the 'cine-eye' and those of Flaherty about the 'participant camera.' I often compare this dynamic improvisation with that of the bullfighter before the bull. In both cases nothing is given in advance, and the smoothness of a *faëna* (strategy of play) in bullfighting is analogous to the harmony of a traveling shot which is in perfect balance with the movements of the subjects.

Here again, it is a question of training, of the kind of mastery of the body that proper gymnastics might allow us to acquire. Then, instead of using the zoom, the cameraman-film maker can really get into his subject, can precede or follow a dancer, a priest, or a craftsman. He is no longer just himself but he is a 'mechanical eye' accompanied by an 'electronic ear.' It is this bizarre state of transformation in the film maker that I have called, by analogy with phenomena of possession, the 'cine-trance'.

Editing

The producer-cameraman of direct cinema is his own first spectator thanks to the viewfinder of his camera. All gestural improvisation (movements, centerings, duration of shots) finally leads to editing in the camera itself. We can note here again the notion of Vertov: 'the "cine-eye" is just this: I EDIT· when I choose my subject [from among the thousands of possible subjects]. I EDIT when I observe [film] my subject [to find the best choice from among a thousand possible observations. . .]' (Vertov).

Actually this work done in the field is what specifically marks the film maker-ethnologist. Instead of waiting until he has returned from the field to elaborate upon his notes, he must try, under threat of failure, to synthesize them at the very moment he observes particular events. He must conduct his cinematic study, alter it or cut it short, while on location. It is no longer a question of cuts written down in advance, nor of cameras determining the order of sequences, but instead it is a sort of risky game in which each shot is determined by the preceding one and itself determines the next. Certainly shooting with synchronous sound demands perfect correlation between the cameraman and the soundman (and the latter who, I repeat, must understand perfectly the language spoken by the people filmed, plays an essential role in this adventure). If this 'cine-eye' and 'cine-ear' crew is well-trained, the technical problems will be resolved by means of simple reflexes (focus, F-stop) and the film maker and his soundman are left free for this spontaneous creation. 'Cine-eye = cine-I see [I see with the camera] + cine-I write [I record on film with the camera] + cine-I organize [I edit]' (Vertov).

During the filming, thanks to the viewfinder and headphones the production crew will immediately know the quality of what has been recorded. They can stop if they aren't satisfied (so as to try another way), or if it is going well, they can continue to connect together the sentences of the story which is created at the very moment that the action transpires. And that is, for me, the real 'participant camera.'

The next spectator is the editor. He must never participate in the filming, but be the second 'cine-eye'; not being acquainted with the context, he must only see and hear what has actually been recorded (whatever the intentions of the film maker might have been). Thus, the editing between the subjective author and the objective editor is a harsh and difficult dialogue, but one on which the whole film depends. Here again, there is no recipe: Association [addition, subtraction, multiplication, division and bracketing together] of film strips of the same sort. Incessant permutation of these pieces of film until they are placed in a rhythmic order in which all of the cues for meaning coincide with all of the visual cues (Vertov).

But there is another step not foreseen by Vertov that seems indispensable to me. This is the presentation of the first rushes ('from beginning to end' in order) to the people who were filmed and whose participation is essential. I will come back to this later.

Commentary, subtitles, music

It is not possible to transmit two auditory messages simultaneously. One will be understood at the expense of the other. The ideal would therefore be a film in which the sound would be the synchronous sound that accompanied the action. Unfortunately, ethnographic films generally present us with complex alien cultures whose people speak an unknown language.

A commentary, as in silent films or a film shown along with a lecture, seems to be the simplest solution; it is the direct discourse of the film maker who becomes the intermediary between self and others. This discourse, which should be subjective, is most often objective. It usually takes the form of a manual or of a scientific exposition which brings together the maximum amount of associated information. So, strangely enough, instead of clarifying the pictures, the film commentary generally obscures and masks them until the words substitute themselves for the pictures. It is no longer a film, but a lecture or a demonstration with an animated visual background. This demonstration should have been made by the images themselves. Rare indeed, then, are ethnographic films whose commentary is the counterpoint of the pictures. I shall cite two examples here: *Terre sans pain* [Land without bread] by Luis Buñuel, in which Pierre Unik's violently subjective text carries the vocal cruelty necessary to sights which are often quite unbearable; and *The Hunters* by John Marshall, in which the film maker leads us with a very simple narrative along the trails of giraffes and their hunters. The film therefore becomes as much the adventures of the hunters and their prey as the adventure of the film maker himself.

When new equipment came into use which allowed shooting with synchronous sound, ethnographic films, like all direct cinema films, became talkative, and the commentary was subjected to the impossible operation of dubbing into another language. More and more, actors were called upon to speak the 'commentary' in the hope of approximating the quality of commercial cinema. The result, with a few rare exceptions, was pitiful. Far from translating, transmitting, and approximating reality, this sort of discourse betrayed the subject and drifted away from reality. Personally, after some bad experiences (American version of *La chasse au lion à l'arc* [The lion hunters]), I have preferred to narrate my own films even with my own bad English accent (e.g. *Les maîtres fous* [The mad masters]).

It would be quite interesting to study the style of the commentaries of ethnographic films since the 1930's. One would note how they passed from a colonial baroque period to one of exotic adventurism, and then on to the dryness of a scientific report. More recently they are characterised either by the shameful distance of anthropologists not wanting to confess their passion for the people they study, or by an ideological discourse through which the film maker exports notions of revolution that he has not been able to act upon in his own country. We would thus obtain both a series of profiles characteristic of various times and places, and insights into the scholars of our discipline that no book or lecture could reveal better.

Titles and subtitles therefore appear to be the most effective means of escaping from the trap of commentary. John Marshall was, in my estimation, the first to use this process in his *Kalahari* series for the Peabody Museum. His very simple film *The Pond* about the chatting and mild flirting of Bushmen around a waterhole remains a model of the genre. The difficulties involved in the procedure must not be discounted, however. Besides mutilating the picture, the most difficult obstacle to overcome is the time needed to read titles. As in commercial cinema, the subtitle can be no more than a condensation of what is said. I tried to use it for a sync-sound film on lion hunters (*Un lion nommé l'Américain* [A Lion called 'the American']). However, it was impossible to transcribe satisfactorily the difficult translation of the essential text (praises of the poisoned arrow) declaimed at the moment of the lion's death, because there was not enough time to read everything. The time needed to hear information is much shorter, so I spoke the text which became a voice-over of the original text. Actually the result is also deceptive, for even if this esoteric text takes on a poetic value at that moment, it offers no complementary information. I have returned today to a version without either commentary or subtitles. In essence it would be quite miraculous to be able to give the audience access to so much knowledge and so many complex techniques in twenty minutes when it requires decades of apprenticeship on the part of the hunters themselves. In these circumstances, the film can only be an open door to this knowledge. It is a free pathway and those who wish to learn more can refer to the short pamphlet (an example of the 'ethnographic companion to film') which should henceforth accompany every ethnographic film.

To complete this discussion of titling and subtitling, I shall mention the excellent effort by Timothy Asch in *The Feast*. In a preamble made up of stills from the principal sequences, the indispensable explanations are given first of all. The film is then discretely titled so as to indicate who is doing what. Of course, this procedure de-mystifies the film from the very beginning, but this is in my estimation the most original effort made so far.

I shall say little about background music. Tape recordings of original music were (and still are) the basis of the soundtracks of most documentary films (and of all the ethnographic films of the 1950's). It was a question here, once more, of 'making movies'. I noticed at a fairly early period (1953) the heresy of this system when I was showing the film *Bataille sur le grand fleuve* [Battle on the great river] to the Nigerian hippopotamus hunters who had been its subjects two years earlier. On the soundtrack I had overlaid the hippopotamus hunt with a quite moving 'hunting air' of string music which had a chase theme. It had seemed to me to be particularly appropriate for this sequence. The result was deplorable; the leader of the hunters asked me to leave out the music since the hunt had to be completely silent . . . Ever since that adventure, I have paid careful attention to the use of music in films, and I am convinced that even in commercial cinema it is a totally theatrical and outdated convention. Music envelops one, can put one asleep, lets bad cuts pass unnoticed or gives artificial rhythm to images which have no rhythm and never will have any. In brief, it is the opium of cinema and, unfortunately, television has exploited the mediocrity of this process. I feel that admirable Japanese ethnographic films such as *Papua, a New Life* and especially *Kula, Argonauts of the Western Pacific* are spoiled by the musical sauce with which they are all served, necessary though it may seem.

On the other hand, we must value music which really supports an action, whether it be profane or ritual music, the rhythm of work or of dance. And although it is beyond the scope of this study, I must note here the considerable importance that the technique of synchronous film has and will have in the area of ethnomusicology.

The editing of sound (whether environment, words, or music) is doubtless just as complex as that of pictures, but here again I believe we must make some real progress and get rid of those prejudices which undoubtedly stem from radio. They result in our treating sound with more respect than we treat pictures. Many recent films of the direct cinema type are thus spoiled by incredible regard for the chatting of the people filmed, as if oral testimony were more sacred than the visual sort. While that kind of film maker will not hesitate at all to cut off a gesture in the middle of a motion, he will never dare cut off a speech in the middle of a sentence or a word. Even less often will he dare cut off a musical theme before its final note. I believe that this archaic habit (which television uses a great deal) will disappear quite soon and that pictures will once again take priority.

The audience of the ethnographic film: films for research and distribution
This last point (a final link which could equally well be the first one of a chain if we were asked to justify our intentions) is in my estimation essential for ethnographic film today. Everywhere—in Africa, in universities, in cultural centers, on television, at the Center for Scientific Research of the *Cinémathèque Française*—the first question that is asked after the screening of an ethnographic film is: 'For whom have you produced this film, and why?'

Why and for whom do we put the camera amongst people? Strangely enough, my first response to this will always be the same: 'For myself.' It isn't that I am addicted to a particular drug whose 'lack' would make itself quite regularly felt, but rather that, at certain times in certain places and around certain people, the camera (and especially the sync-sound camera) seems to be necessary. Of course, it will always be possible to justify its use for scientific reasons (the creation of audiovisual archives of cultures which are rapidly changing or in danger of disappearing), or political ones (sharing in a revolt against an intolerable situation), or aesthetic ones (discovery of a fragile masterpiece in a landscape, a face, or a gesture that we simply cannot let fade away unrecorded). But actually, we make a certain film because there is suddenly that necessity to film, or in some quite similar circumstances, a certainty that filming must not occur.

Perhaps our frequenting of cinema theaters and our ill-timed use of audio-visual methods might make some of us into mad *kinokis* in Vertov's sense or into 'cine-eyes' like the 'pen-hands' (Rimbaud) of earlier times who could not keep from writing: '... I was there..., such-and-such a thing happened to me...' (La Fontaine). If the cine-voyeur of his own society could always justify himself by this sort of militancy, what reason could we as anthropologists give for the glances we cast over the wall at others?

Without a doubt, this word of interrogation must be addressed to all anthropologists, but none of their books or articles has ever been questioned as much as have anthropological films. And that would be my second response: film is the only method I have to show another just how I see him. In other words, for me, my prime audience is (after the pleasure of the 'cine-trance' during the filming and editing) the other person, the one I am filming.

So the position is much clearer: henceforth, the anthropologist has at his disposal the only tool—the 'participant camera'—which can provide him with the extraordinary opportunity to communicate with the group under study. He has the film that he made about them. Admittedly we do not yet have all of the technical keys to this, and projection of a film in the field is still at an experimental stage. Without a doubt, the perfection of an automatic super-8 sound projector which runs on a 12-volt battery will be an important step forward, but the experiments that I have been able to carry out with a rebuilt 16mm projector and a small portable 300-watt generator have already proved conclusive: the projection of the film *Sigui 69* in the village of Bongo where it was shot brought considerable reaction from the Dogon of the Bandiagara cliffs together with a request for more films, a series of which is now being made there. The projection of a film called *Horendi* on the initiation rites of possessed dancers in Niger has allowed me, by studying the film on a viewer with priests who had participated in the ritual, to gather more information in a fortnight than I could get from three months of direct observation and interviews with the same informants. And here again we were asked to make more films. This *a posteriori* information on film is still only in its early stages, but it is already producing completely new relationships between the anthropologist and the group he is studying. This is the start of what some of us are already calling 'shared anthropology'. The observer is finally coming down from his ivory tower; his camera, his tape recorder, and his projector have led him—by way of a strange initiation path—to the very heart of knowledge and, for the first time, his work is not being judged by a thesis committee but by the very people he came to observe.

This extraordinary technique of 'feedback' (which I translate as 'audiovisual counter-gift') has certainly not yet revealed all of its possibilities, but we can see already that, thanks to feedback, the anthropologist is no longer an entomologist observing his subject as if it were an insect (putting it down) but rather as if it were a stimulant for mutual understanding (hence dignity).

This sort of research employing total participation, idealistic though it may be, seems to me to be the only morally and scientifically possible anthropological attitude today. Today's camera designers should try their hardest to further the development of its technical aspects (super-8 and videotape).

But it would obviously be absurd to condemn ethnographic film to this closed circuit of audiovisual information. This is why my third response to that question 'For whom?' is: 'For the greatest number of people possible, for all audiences.' I believe that if the distribution of our ethnographic films is limited (except for rare exceptions) to a select network of universities, learned societies, and cultural organs, it is due less to the wide distribution of commercial films than it is to a fault in the films that we are producing. It is time for ethnographic films to become cinema in their own right.

I do not think that this is impossible as long as their essential quality of being the privileged records of one or two individuals can be carefully preserved. If lectures by explorers and if television series done in travelogue style have been successful, it is only because—and I repeat this—behind the clumsily taken shots there lurks the presence of the person who took them. As long as an anthropologist-film maker, out of scientism or ideological shame, hides himself behind a comfortable sort of incognito, he will ruin his films irreparably and they will join the documents in archives which only the specialists see. Recently ethnographic works, which had previously been reserved for a very small group of scientific libraries, have been published in paperback editions. Their success gives the ethnographic film maker an example to follow.

While waiting for the production of real ethnographic films, i.e. films which, according to the obvious definition we gave them nearly twenty years ago, 'tie cinematic language to scientific rigor,' the International Committee for Ethnographic and Sociological Film decided, at the last Venice film festival (Venezia Genti 1972) to create a veritable network of conservation, documentation, and distribution of 'the films of man,' with the aid of UNESCO. For we are people who believe that the world of tomorrow, this world we are now in the process of building, will only be viable if it recognizes the differences among various cultures and if we do not deny the existence of these cultures by trying to transform them into images of ourselves. In order to achieve this, we must know these other cultures; to acquire this knowledge, there is no better tool than ethnographic film.

This is not a pious vow, for an example comes to us from the Far East. A Japanese television company, hoping to bring the Japanese out of their insularity, decided to broadcast once a week, for three years, an hour of ethnographic film.

Conclusion: shared cinema-anthropology

Here we are at the end of our survey of the various uses of the camera among men of yesterday and today. The only conclusion that can be drawn at this point is that ethnographic film has not even passed through its experimental stages yet, and that, while anthropologists have a fabulous tool at their disposal, they do not yet know how to use it properly.

At this stage there are no 'schools of ethnographic film'; only trends. Personally, I hope that this marginal situation will last for a while to avoid freezing a young discipline into immutable norms and to keep it from developing a sterile bureaucracy. It is good that American, Canadian, Japanese, Brazilian, Australian, Dutch, British, and French ethnographic films are so different. We can contrast this multiplicity of conception with the universality of concepts characteristic of the scientific approach. If the 'cine-eyes' of all countries are ready to unite, it is not to create a universal point of view. I have already stated that films of human science are, in a certain sense, in the forefront of cinematic research. In the diversity of recent films, similar tendencies are appearing because our experiments have led to the same conclusions in different places. The multiplication of shot sequences is new, (and I have asked a designer of light cameras to produce a 16mm 1000-feet magazine which will permit continuous filming for half an hour). We are thus giving birth to a new filmic language.

And tomorrow? Tomorrow will be the day of the self-regulating color videotape, of automatic video editing, of 'instant replay' of the recorded picture (immediate feedback). The dreams of Vertov and Flaherty will be combined into a mechanical 'cine-eye-ear' which is such a 'participant' camera that it will pass automatically into the hands of those who were, up to now, always in front of it. Then the anthropologist will no longer monopolize the observation of things. Instead, both he and his culture will be observed and recorded. In this way ethnographic film will help us 'share' anthropology.

63

CINEMA AND SOCIOLOGY

Thoughts on Chronique d'un été

Lucien Goldmann

Editorial note: *Lucien Goldmann's article can be seen as a sample of the characteristic response from academic sociology to Rouch/Morin's film. Goldmann focuses on whether the methodology of the film is consonant with the methodology of sociological enquiry. Briefly, he maintains that sociology is concerned with concepts while film deals with individuals. According to this argument, a film such as* Chronique *can thus at best be granted the status of an 'immediate', that is to say, an unmediated document, of interest and use only if contained by and explicated from a body of theory outside of the film itself.*
    This article was first published in Le Cinéma et la Vérité, *a special issue of* Artsept, *1963, edited by Raymond Bellour. The translation is by John Higgins.*

The film by Edgar Morin and Jean Rouch poses a series of questions which are the transposition of the fundamental problems which engage the whole of modern sociology onto the sphere of cinematic realisation, and it seems to me that these questions can be usefully raised, even in the very general perspective of a recollection already several months old.

Basically, the problem is the methodological value of unguided or barely directed interviews and clinical conversations as means of access to the knowledge of human reality. For, at the risk of speaking rather simplistically, we have to point out that Morin and Rouch's film is only the recording onto the screen of a sum of interviews and several individual exchanges which are rather simplified by the limits imposed by the projection time. It should be stressed that not only does this judgement concern the several sequences where two girls are walking around with a microphone, putting questions to passers-by in the street, but the whole of the film as well, which is made up of similar conversations between the producers and the protagonists, and several collective discussions.

The basic objections to any sociological research based solely on conversation and the questionnaire are well known. 'The truth is the whole' said Hegel. Now, conversation and questionnaires are precisely partial fragments, not inserted into global structures, and which, on that account, remain no less abstract, even when they are concerned with authentic and lived cases (which are the best cases), and, consequently, are extremely poor in relation to the much richer and more complex structure of reality. The same awakening in a bachelor's bedroom, the same breakfast brought in by the mother, can have a rigorously different signification according to the global context in which these acts are situated. Now, the sociologist can eventually grasp this context with the help of conceptual and structural research, but, as for the film maker, who does not have the possibility of filming concepts, he can only seize it through its reproduction at the level of individual beings and concrete situations which are the only things directly available to him: which is to say, on the level of fiction.

Of course, fiction always risks being arbitrary and the problem which seems to have been the root of Morin and Rouch's preoccupations was precisely to avoid the arbitrary, to grasp actual reality, to get the truth. But precisely at this point, we fear that they have come up against a major methodological difficulty which was long since pointed out in the methodological works of Hegel and Marx: when it's a question of human realities, the truth is never immediate, and anything which is immediate remains abstract and, for that very reason, stained by inexactitude as long as it is not inserted into the whole by a number of more or less large and complex mediations. Morin and Rouch were in fact aware of this problem and did their best to try and deal with the difficulties we have just mentioned by replacing the usual cast of the questionnaire or sociological dialogue, randomly picked, by people whom they knew quite well, and whose global co-ordinates they could then implicitly utilise.

There is in this an undeniable methodological benefit for the film maker who, in such a case, knows best the questions to be asked and also, the way they should be put in order to obtain characteristic and significant replies. In this sense, *Chronique d'un été* went quite a long way within the limits permitted by such a method.

But it remains no less true that the co-ordinates of the characters, known to Morin and Rouch, are not known to the viewers and on that account, the film becomes much more abstract and much less significant for the latter, even though familiarisation with the distorting data given and transmitted by most of the messages of contemporary culture and pseudo-culture prevent an awareness of that.

Finally, as in all the problems touching on art and human realities, there is no unilateral and universal solution which is valid. As a means of access to as rigorous a knowledge as possible of reality, the fiction film contains extremely grave dangers, but at the same time it contains possibilities correspondent to those dangers. Again, inquiry and conversation, when they are honestly employed, with no intention of deceit or propaganda—that is undoubtedly the case with Morin and Rouch's film—present of course, on the level of immediate recording, a major guarantee of authenticity; on the other hand, they offer greatly reduced possibilities of access to the true structure of reality, and, because of that, to the significance of the facts they are recording. What then is the solution? We have just said that it could only be dialectical: it is the balance which in each particular case has to be renewed between, on the one hand, a global framework which can only be imaginary but which can be elaborated from as objective a preliminary sociological research as is possible, and, on the other hand, exactitude in the reproduction of the partial elements.

In the final analysis I would be willing to say that, given the method used, Morin and Rouch have probably obtained everything it was possible to obtain in a first attempt and that, in this sense, their film undeniably represents a partial success and an important document. But precisely to the extent that it clearly reveals the principle methodological problems posed by cinema vérité. The use of the camera: in relation to science, for the recording of immediate data of a documentary nature, and in relation to aesthetics, for the creation of a work of fiction. In relation to science: equivalence to reality is called truth. In aesthetics, it is called realism. But scientific truth is never in the immediate document, even though it can't do without it. In this domain, the camera could only then furnish more precise information for a global scientific analysis, and cinema vérité is only possible inside a theoretical development which the image alone could not get across. Again, the cinema has no autonomy in relation to equivalence with reality except in so far as it wishes to be seen as a means of aesthetic creation. Which is to say that at the same time as acknowledging the value of the experience and testimony represented by Morin and Rouch's film, we are afraid that right from the start it is very close to the limits of this kind of film, and that scientific truth, cinematic realism and aesthetic value are precisely beyond these limits.

As an end to these reflections, let us add, however, that our reservations concerning Morin and Rouch's film, developed from quite rigid require-ments, not only concerns the film itself and the cinematic technique involved, but above all, the inherent difficulties of both sociological research and aesthetic creation in contemporary industrial society. It's not chance that the objections we have just pointed out about *Chronique d'un été* are just as valid for eighty per cent of the research done by contemporary sociology, which, even when the results are presented in the form of a book in which conceptual concerns could be introduced, do not get that far, and do not get above the level of the immediate document. In the same way it's no accident that the praiseworthy concern which moved Morin and Rouch to make *Chronique d'un été*, implies a justified criticism of a very large number of imaginative works which lose all contact with reality, while at the same time posing as realist works.

Truth, realism, coherence and aesthetic unity are values whose attainment is not, these days, a simple problem of good faith, effort, talent, or even individual genius. It is also, and in the first instance, the problem of the difficulties and limits which a cultural milieu brings to bear on the products of the mind. A work has to be judged both in relation to the author's project and in relation to the intellectual difficulties inherent in that time. From this point of view, *Chronique d'un été* certainly remains an interesting and symptomatic document which deserves to be singled out from amongst the experimental attempts of contemporary cinema.

66

SLIPPAGES OF FICTION

Some notes on the cinema of Jean Rouch

Jean-André Fieschi

Editorial note: Fieschi's article, the most intelligent appraisal of Rouch's work published to date, points out that Rouch's cinema is not reducible to the categories of either the ethnographic film or the classic fiction film, but that it occupies, within fiction, a space of its own with its own specific effectivity.

   This article was written for Cinema: A Critical Dictionary, *edited by Richard Roud, to be published shortly by Martin Secker & Warburg Ltd. A French version was published in a special issue of the* Revue d'Esthetique, *edited by D. Noguez, entitled* Cinéma, Théories, Lectures *(1973).*

A survey of Jean Rouch's career in films, which now covers over twenty-five years, from the first ethnological shorts to *Petit à Petit*, suggests that what gives his work its novelty, elasticity and disruptive power lies chiefly in the discomfort it effects, using any means to attain its ends, resorting to different techniques venturing into hitherto uncharted areas, mingling devices previously believed to be contradictory, and refusing to be confined by any established facts.

   Truant ethnology, one is tempted to say of the African side of Rouch's work. A dunce directing (by comparison with the studious pupils: Rosi, Melville, Losey...) when he gets into more deliberately fictional areas: neglectful of the prescribed rules, and even rather priding himself on finding ways round them. Above all, though, contraband cinema, with Rouch ever ready to cross frontiers which he himself seems to have set up for himself. Hence the misunderstandings accumulated during his travels: unacceptable, this rather too whimsical ethnologist too fond of chasing butterflies; incongruous, this film maker unacquainted with continuity, dramatic construction, rounded characters.

   What is exploded by Rouch's work (with the result that, rather as Boulez said of music after Debussy, the entire cinema now 'breathes' differently) is the whole system of statutory oppositions whereby, starting from the original Lumière-Méliès axis, categories were conceived of as documentary/ficton; style/improvisation; natural/artificial; etc.

   Certainly there was a succession of tremors before Rouch—Vertov, Flaherty, Rossellini—clearly indicating the inanity of these traditional academic oppositions. But Rouch gave the extra turn of the screw that proved decisive. For a time, any real evaluation was avoided by falling back on the absurdly muddle headed term *cinema vérité*, loosely borrowed from

Dziga Vertov and his 'Kino Pravda'. During the sixties, an interminable debate on the subject cluttered festivals, film magazines and conferences. Usually a suspect ideology of artlessness (the transparency of reality, intensified by the 'miracle' of direct sound and the myth of natural expression by the film maker and his characters) took care of the problem of an artificiality as extreme as in any Hollywood movie though on a different level and achieved by different means. The rival schools weighed in with disputes in which everybody—Rossellini, Leacock, the Canadians—accused everybody else of cheating, laziness or illusionism. An undeniable fact today is that although Rouch took part in the debate, he did so without taking sides except as the spoilsport who exposed its inherent falseness.

'Anything could happen here': this phrase, spoken at the beginning of *Shanghai Gesture*, is a sort of 'open sesame' to Sternberg's aesthetic. It suggests a mental locus subject to substitutions, transformations, metamorphoses, marvels. If one wants to define the components of Rouch's work, one must look to Sternberg's narrative myths, Cocteau's poetic wonderland, the speculative flights of surrealism. Or to the story-teller spinning a yarn while wide eyed children listen with bated breath: 'Listen, children, for goodness' sake.' This is how the tale begins of a lion hunt with bows and arrows, apparently in Africa but really in some strange country beyond 'the bush which is far further than far away, the land of nowhere'. After 'the mountains of the moon', the 'mountains of crystal'. . .

Each time a frontier must be crossed, or a mirror traversed, to reach that elsewhere or other world on which dreams and stories feed. Each film becomes an account of an initiation ceremony. Here the determining factors of the ethnologist's life—his desire, in fact—must be considered. Claude Lévi-Strauss (and Michel Leiris [in *L'Afrique fantôme*]), is enlightening in this respect: 'The conditions of his life and work cut him off from his own group for long periods; and he himself acquires a kind of chronic uprootedness from the sheer brutality of the environmental changes to which he is exposed. Never can he feel himself "at home" anywhere.' (Lévi-Strauss, *Tristes tropiques*.)

In Rouch's early efforts, the camera, a supplementary tool in the ethnologist's equipment affording greater accuracy and flexibility, recorded rites and customs: those of the men who make rain, the millet people, the sorcerers of Wanzerbe. A tool recommended by Mauss, Leroi-Gourhan, Marcel Griaule, and even by pioneers like Dr Regnault as early as 1900. A 'scientific' tool capable, according to them, of avoiding or correcting undue subjectivity in the observer. And one not even indulging in selectivity.

So Rouch, in the early fifties, was recording rites, customs and techniques because 'If young ethnographers are well advised to favour rituals and techniques as subjects for filming, it is because rituals and techniques incorporate their own *mise en scène*.'

This kind of cinema, dependent upon the event, the moment, the place, is of course not *written*, not created. What is created, unexpectedly, as it unfolds within the framework of a scenario determined in advance but

68

irrespective of the film maker, is the cultural form of the ceremony recorded. The film maker here is the *operator* (in Mallarmé's sense of control mechanism, distributor of signs, as well as in the strictly technical sense of cameraman): eye glued to the viewfinder, framing for the rectangle an elusive, ephemeral performance—he himself being its first spectator—dependent not only on his cultural prejudices but on his reflexes, his speed, his patience, the very movements of his body which transmit slight tremors, jolts or stoppages to the camera. Movements by the camera, length of takes, variations in light, the grain of the film stock: usually nullified in 'scientific' films by the thesis which takes charge and the information that is offered, all the technical hazards through which matter is filtered and transformed (and which allow it to resist) are brought into the foreground for the first time in Rouch's work. On an equal footing, one might almost say, with the subject represented.

This discovery in practice of the *materiality* of the cinema itself was probably an important determining factor for Rouch: a materiality whereby the scientific statement of the evidence, slightly dislocated, becomes the fluctuating expression of an elusive subjectivity that is simultaneously present and withdrawn even as it is being formulated.

For instance, the group of short films presented under the collective title of *Les fils de l'eau* describing various aspects of the lives of tribesmen along the banks of the Niger: prayers for rain, the coming of the rain, the sowing and harvesting of millet, burial rites, circumcision, a hippopotamus hunt. Images apparently without frills, as though shot by any member of the crew who happened to be on hand, a commentary derived directly from the local dialect (in sentence structure, the incantatory manner, the repetition and variation of simple words), and tribal chants and music all combine to create the illusion—at times perfect—of a total absence of white men. A direct attempt to penetrate an alien mentality simply by describing faces, gestures and everyday objects.

But the voice which takes charge of these images, carrying them along and seeming to direct their flow as much as to submit to them, is the voice of Rouch. The captivating voice of the narrator, the story-teller, the barker who tells you in his own warm and persuasive way that we shall see what we shall see. A voice which mirrors the action rather than explaining or commenting on it, withdrawn from the images and 'charging' them.

Les hommes de la pluie: the earth is parched, the harvest threatened. Only magic practices can restore fertility. These practices are enumerated, described, demonstrated. And when the black sky opens in the final shots and the rain pours down inundating the dry and cracking earth, the expected miracle is literally realised, a relationship of cause and effect is established between the rite and its reward. The film thus seems to accept the miracle, even to stand as evidence of it. Hazy and disquieting, the washed-out, uneven colour, unlike any other (Godard wanted at one time to use it for *Les carabiniers*: neither glowing Technicolor nor so-called 'natural' colour), accentuates the effect of strangeness.

69

To the illusion of the absence of white men is added the illusion of the absence of any manipulation in the filmed material (one never for a moment thinks of what might have been cut during editing; on the contrary, the impression one gets is that each scene is presented exactly as it was shot, breaking off only when the camera runs out of film or the observer out of interest), while at the same time an insistent presence—the voice—effects a displacement, suggesting that the spectacle we are watching comes unmistakably within the province of the fantasy film, the domain of science fiction.

The fantastic element is in fact twofold; hence its particular effectiveness. Bound up with the 'elsewhere' made manifest, the quizzical otherness, so close and yet so far, there is the strangeness of what we see, defined as such solely by cultural differences; and there is the narrative method, unimpeachable in its logical sequence, introducing the fantastic along with an unfamiliar causality. And enhancing these powers, as is right and proper, there is every semblance of innocence, of simply stated fact: You see how it is ...

Clearly this innocence derives from an ideology of immediacy, the intangible sense of actual experience, which Rouch claims as automatism, inspiration, even manifestation: 'What are these films, what outlandish name distinguishes them from the rest? Do they exist? I have no idea as yet, but I do know that there are certain very rare occasions when, without the aid of a single subtitle, the spectator suddenly understands an unknown tongue, takes part in strange ceremonies, wanders in towns or through landscapes he has never seen but which he recognizes perfectly ... Only the cinema can perform this miracle, though no particular aesthetic can reveal the mechanism, and no special technique can set it in motion: neither clever counterpointing in the cutting, nor the use of some stereophonic cinerama process can create such wonders ...'

And further on: 'It is as if there were no more cameras, no more sound recorders, no more photo-electric cells, none of the welter of accessories and technicians which comprise the great ritual of classic cinema. But the film makers of today prefer not to venture into these dangerous paths; and only fools, madmen and children dare to push the fobidden buttons.'

This article (*Positif*, November, 1955) is a veritable mine, in that it is a fairly clear indication of how the scientific purpose was deflected in favour of the camera, at first only the instrument of revelation but suddenly given special licence. Look again at each of the assumptions and expressions in Rouch's chain of thought, so strikingly tinged with the tone of poetic revelation: privileged moment, communication without intermediaries, taking part in a ceremony, sense of recognition, miracle, wonders, dangerous paths, fools, madmen and children ...

There is no point in using this manifesto to query the scientific basis of Rouch's approach, but it is clear that from the outset cinema and science acted for him as pretexts—or rather, generators—for each other. The relationship to be sought is therefore not primarily between a science (ethnological) and a given technique (in this case the technique of cinema, required to transmit this science through a specific medium), which is why film makers and ethnologists get so little out of Rouch's work, a sort of double agent cinema operating more broadly between science and fiction (of course Rouch's films can also be described, without too much play on words, as science fiction).

Straddling techniques, straddling cultures, Rouch (ostensibly for pragmatic reasons) was to play increasingly systematically on this betwixt-and-between which he made the mainspring of a long, profoundly original, and extremely influential fictional cycle. Progressively, too, he complicated the game. At this point may be noted Rouch's relationship with his film making predecessors: Vertov he praises as a director 'of films which beget films'; Flaherty is a 'Jack-of-all-trades, a man of action and a poet,' but above all 'a *metteur en scène*, one of the greatest'.

No matter how acute the sense of dislocation, his first films bearing witness to 'the marvellous African' still took a relatively classical reportage form. What is new about *Les fils de l'eau* and the cycle it inaugurates, by comparison with the indistinguishable mass of ethnological films, is the tone, the manifest presence of an aesthetic; and the difference between his footage and traditional factual reports, as projected on the screen, is above all a qualitative one: the information is there, but woven as it were into a texture which modifies, indeed transforms, its character and function. A takeover is effected on the discourse, a recognisable stamp placed on it, a scenic quality, the hand of a film maker.

With *Les maîtres fous* comes a first, though still hesitant, edging towards more open forms, more disturbing structures: structures in which the disturbing element, the frontier crossed somewhere, is integral to their functioning. The film describes the great annual ceremony of the Hauka, or demons of power, in Ghana. Rouch is no longer simply recording a ritual, but making a more complex survey of an essentially cathartic collective practice, a sacrifice whose exceptional nature is clearly understood to be an assurance of social normality. As in every fantasy film, this 'normality' is established at the outset, and functions as the *alter ego* or double of the bloody sacred ceremony. The characters come from ordinary, everyday life, urban this time. There is nothing unusual about them at home or at work: labourers, waiters, workers. Then, during the ceremony (followed in detail, step by step), they become literally possessed, alienated, foaming, mixing the blood of dogs and the yolks of eggs, drunk on slaughtered animals, streaming with spittle, contorted. Afterwards, reclaimed by their (non-sacred) social context, they return to normal until the next sacrifice. This first reversal of everyday reality and the sacrificial ritual is suddenly punctuated by incongruous red and green images: the changing of the Horse Guards against a lush prairie background.

Although the message is obvious in the ingenuous directness with which the supposed civilised and savage states are grafted to the same stem, and although an exercise like this basically reveals little but banalities, a powerful

71

element of surprise nevertheless comes into play, less on the level of the discourse than on that of the film as fiction: a metaphorical disorientation, born of another space-time (of other narrative and cultural systems indicating the course of colonisation) and imposing a second dislocation on the already disturbing dislocation which seemed to be the subject of the film. Here the reading system is geared down. The exploration of cinema as source material rich in possibilities other than simply transitive is succeeded by the exploration of cinema as structure (narrative, poetic, plastic, critical). A combinative is suggested between the basic data which the cinema (because of the nature of its relationship to reality) has brought into play since its very beginnings: reality and its characteristic resistance to let itself be inscribed within a frame, to submit to techniques which are inevitably constricting; and everything that the logic of concrete selection engenders as possibilities for new juxtapositions, and for modifying the raw material filmed (even when this is given data from the outset, already *mise en scène*, as in the case of the ritual or ceremony).

Rouch was to work on this given/manipulation relationship, surveying its possibilities charting hitherto unexplored junctures, so that his influence on the cinema then developing or searching for ways and means was probably greater than any other (on Godard, Rivette, and even, though one might not at first think so, on Straub).

One can see how the terms applied to elders like Vertov and Flaherty came to be revived in connection with his work.

What Rouch's practice of ethnographical cinema revealed was a corpus of repudiations rather similar, after due historical adjustment, to the one vented by Vertov in the euphoria of a new world requiring new forms: 'It was at the time when the outlines of the Kino Eye movement were just beginning to take shape, when we had to decide whether we were going to follow in the footsteps of the art cinema and make products of cine-distillation like the entire fraternity of film makers—an occupation both lucrative and sanctioned by law—or whether we were going to declare war on the art cinema and start to rebuild the cinema from scratch. Puppets or life? we asked the spectator . . .'

A corpus of repudiations equally concerned with actors and acting, text, decor, classical montage and methods of *découpage*, with what Bresson was to describe as caricature, and Straub as pornography. In this Rouch was to be one of the great gold miners of the contemporary cinema. Taking a course directly opposed to Richard Leacock's counterfeit journalistic practice of supposed non-intervention, he worked on processes, inter-actions, mutual discovery between matter and method, film and discourse. Reality never offers itself as such to the innocent eye or virgin celluloid. What reality, anyway?

One might perhaps hazard that the movement of Rouch's work at this point is increasingly obviously directed towards the fictional, the imaginary already realised, in the early films dealing with rituals, but progressively, differently encompassed and revealed; increasingly dependent upon a system of representation less direct than that of simple reportage, incorporating the element of fabrication proper to every system of representation, not to mention the discreet but central parts played by the observer who harvests the fiction and by the technical means which bring it to its completed theatrical form as the product of successive deposits deriving from various systems (the social and cultural system in which the original representation took place, the system into which it is received, the cultural and technical system through which it is transmitted). This is Rouch's cinema: the repository for a particularly complex network of transitions and displacements through which one arrives at a different and richer reading of the remark by Lévi-Strauss concerning the self-imposed exile of the ethnologist: 'Never can he feel himself "at home" anywhere.' Actually, this is the only sense in which Rouch can be described as an exotic film maker. Exotic, undoubtedly; but only for the African aspect of his work?

Moi, un noir (1959) clearly states the question at issue in this dislocation: who, in other words, is 'speaking'? The film calling itself by this title? The film maker ironically flaunting his difference? One of his characters? This time, at all events it is a monologue we are invited to watch, to listen to; or rather, a tissue of monologues uniting into a single flow made up of a sum of differences. The characters: real (they exist, you might run into them at Abidjan, for instance), but also dual personalities, with behind them the mythical figures they themselves have chosen (Dorothy Lamour, or Eddie Constantine–Lemmy Caution–American federal agent, or Sugar Ray Robinson).

What Rouch then films, he is the first to attempt: not just behaviour, or dreams, or subjective themes, but the indissoluble amalgam binding them together. The film maker's desire it to devote himself to the desire of his characters. To follow them step by step, along the basic lines of Zavattini's neorealist principle, but with the sights set on what their speech reveals at least as much as on their behaviour. Embodying their disappointments, their daydreams, their desires. The war in Indo-China mimed by one; the liners another indicates in the harbour as he says he's knocked around the seven seas and had his fill of women; the monologue by the ladies' man; the brawl provoked with the Italian: unforgettable moments which reflect films the characters have seen, comic strips they have read, stories they have been told, and which they refashion with inimitable charm into a new narrative. Here all distinction between premeditation and improvisation seems to be abolished, *as though* a transparency between thought and representation were now possible.

Collective creation, improvisation, spontaneity, complicity: these are probably the prime means through which Rouch, the observer of rituals, crossed the line to become a creator of rituals in his own right.

Moi, un noir is undoubtedly a turning point in Rouch's work. In the cinema, in fact. Telling us more about Treichville and its inhabitants than many a seemingly more 'objective' report. Telling us more, but above all, telling us differently.

In *Les maîtres fous*, the members of the sect themselves created the *mise en scène* for their collective delirium in which, decked out in the imaginary regalia of figures symbolising colonialism (the governor, the general, the corporal, the engine driver), they proceeded to enact an imaginary representation that is simultaneously 'wild' and 'ordered'. From *Moi, un noir* onwards, the camera assumes an entirely new function: no longer simply a recording device, it becomes a *provocateur*, a stimulant, precipitating situations, conflicts, expeditions that would otherwise never have taken place. It is no longer a matter of pretending that the camera isn't there, but of transforming its role by asserting its presence, by stressing the part it plays, by turning a technical obstacle into a pretext for revealing new and astonishing things. A matter of creating, through the very act of filming itself, an entirely new conception of the notion of the filmic event. First, with Rouch's camera either leading or tracking them, these inhabitants of Treichville played out what they had chosen to reveal of themselves before it. Then, after seeing themselves on the screen, they commented on the proceedings, reshaping or reorienting them. These successive operations engender a complex cultural object, opening the way to a virtually unexplored avenue: adventure films in which the adventure lies in the material and its discovery. An experimental cinema. A cinema, above all, in which the positions traditionally assigned to the director, technical crew and actors are reassigned and redefined. Film maker/camera operator (when he wasn't behind the camera, as in *Chronique d'un été* or *Les veuves de quinze ans*, 1964—though *Gare du Nord*, 1965, is an exception—the result is a distinct loss, an atypical sense of embarrassment and awkwardness), actors/creators: the arrangement encourages improvisation on many levels. 'When I'm making a film, it takes a few minutes getting started, then I see the film taking shape in the viewfinder of my camera, and I know at any given moment whether what I'm getting is any good or not. The constant tension is exhausting, but it's an excitement absolutely essential if one is to bring off this aleatory pursuit of the most effective images and sounds, without ever being certain until you're shooting the final sequences what the result will be ... Oh, the number of unfinished films I've made because nothing happened—a ritual possession dance in which nobody got possessed; because it grew dark; because I ran out of film ...'

At this point, rather than a panorama of Rouch's work, the fundamental principle on which it is based should perhaps be described in some of its characteristics; characteristics, moreover, which interact on each other to a point where a veritable method—and an extremely coherent one—is discernible behind the flaunted empiricism of his technique.

A method which might equally well be described as a trap, or system of traps: for events, reports, fictions, metamorphoses. Because it is through the diversity of forms, figures and loci annexed by this technique in the course of its adventurous progress—even in its vagaries, its seesawing between techniques and cultures—that a genuine aesthetic is established, with its own laws and practices.

74

An aesthetic whose literary associations are obvious, and which appears to derive entirely from the surrealist principle of spontaneous juxtaposition. This meeting, like two chemical bodies acting upon each other, precipitates a new reality, irreducible to the simple sum of its parts. In literature, André Breton's *Nadja* and Louis Aragon's *Le paysan de Paris* are key examples. But in Rouch's films the incidence of poetry is no longer simply transmitted but created, provoked by the camera.

Jaguar, for instance, records a hazardous quest, a succession of ordeals, a sort of odyssey collectively invented in the course of a methodical, delirious improvisation. Hardly surprising, then, that in what was originally intended to be a report on migration in Ghana, there was talk at one point during the creative euphoria of filming of introducing a dragon or some other monster. In the end the idea was not pursued, and here one undoubtedly has one of the keys to the enterprise: where to stop when documentary actuality is transgressed in favour of another, more complex reality in which the part played by the imaginary is no longer merely ornamental or subordinate, but genuinely basic? Where to stop, too, when the traditional dramatic time scale no longer applied? In other words, at what arbitrary moment should the experience be interrupted, according to what criteria should any particular episode be cut down or entirely excluded during the montage, when the whole richness of the experience lies precisely in the lack of any dramatic censorship, when the meaning lies as much in the erratic course of the narrative as in the content of individual scenes?

Thus we find films running for several hours (*Jaguar* and its sequel *Petit à Petit*), veritable modern serials as crammed with incident as *Les Vampires*, *The Perils of Pauline* or *The Daredevils of the Red Circle*. This radical renovation of cinematographic fiction, drawing on the very earliest sources, results in a change of direction for Rouch, a total reorientation from his original ethnographic position towards films of pure fiction, 'European' films, of which the best and most characteristic is probably his sketch in *Paris vu par . . ., Gare du Nord*.

To describe *Gare du Nord* as characteristic of Rouch's work, almost central to it, as I am tempted to do, may seem surprising: a Parisian film, a fiction film, a *directed* film, whereas Rouch's work seems to derive its charm and its disruptive power from the more exotic elements of ethnology, darkest Africa, improvisation, seeing how others live.

The fact is that with *Gare du Nord*, the questions 'What is Rouch the ethnologist after?' and 'What is Rouch the film maker after?' receive answers which are perhaps less ambiguous and evasive than they seem. Depending upon whether one sees this film as an interlude, an exercise, a *tour de force*, or as an absolutely inevitable development (being already faintly adumbrated in the early films, and vividly present in the later ones), Rouch's *oeuvre* is defined either as eclectic, or as a unity of contradictions whose richness springs from the interaction of these contradictions. What is *Gare du Nord* saying through its incredibly precipitous little tragedy? What is being demonstrated? Who or what is speaking? Probably simply the fascination of the frontier, the breaking point: the record of a dream, a utopia, a reality lost in—and by—the impulse which affirms it.

All the techniques of 'direct' filming are employed and pushed to extremes (synchronous sound, technical mobility, extended takes), but transposed: here the dialogue is written, the locations preselected, the action determined. The enterprise of Hitchcock's *Rope* is renewed: to achieve a coincidence of real time with shooting time, reinforced by the illusion of a single twenty minute take with the reel-change masked by a momentary darkness. 'As far as the dialogue and situations are concerned,' Rouch said, 'there is no question of improvisation, but for the director, crew and actors' performances the improvisation is total.' Emphatically fictional, *Gare du Nord* is a critical riposte to pseudo '*cinema vérité*'. The prolixity, the digressions, the 'dossier' aspect are superseded by an astonishing effect of condensation.

In the film a young couple quarrel one morning in their apartment near the Gare du Nord. She reproaches him for his apathy, his lack of romance, his lack of ambition, and talks of Adventure, of Escape. He half heartedly defends himself. Finally she says he is pitiful, slams the door, and goes down to the street, where she is nearly knocked down by a car. The driver gets out, runs after her to apologise, and offers her Adventure and Escape in precisely the terms she used herself. Then, just as they are crossing a bridge over the railway line, he faces her with a startling bargain: he has decided to kill himself, but if she will go with him, he won't do it. Otherwise, he will throw himself off the bridge. Falteringly, she refused. Instantly, while she stands there, incredulous and shaken, he hurls himself over the bridge on to the railway line below.

This situation, revealed by a hyper-mobile camera hugging close to the tragedy that is evolving, with the experience lived by the characters coinciding exactly with the space–time unit carved out on the screen (Godard spoke of how 'seconds reinforce seconds; when they really pile up, they begin to be impressive'), imposes a dramatic texture reaching almost suffocating heights of intensity until the final fall (in more than one sense of the word) on the brink of a void (mental, physical) which is less a conclusion than what the film is all about.

Formal suspense and dramatic suspense are inextricably linked here in a synthesising conception of technique. The constant modification of the frame, obedient to Nadine's wilful movements, subjected to the grainy uncertainty of a bluish light, assailed by waves of city sounds, defines a hallucinating odyssey in which, momentarily, as she parts from her husband, the dream of 'elsewhere' is adumbrated before being suddenly, brutally transformed into the more radical parting of death, whereupon the frame opens out to efface the characters it had hitherto clung to so feverishly.

Surely it is impossible not to see here the affirmation of an aesthetic, with the ethnological 'elsewhere', assimilated into the imaginary space between three people, suddenly and retrospectively realising its function? It was in *Gare du Nord* that the repeatedly shifting frontiers of adventure, dreams, illusion—and also of direct cinema and *mise en scène*—revealed themselves as the object of an itinerary which is only seemingly capricious, and which gambles on this capriciousness as its essence.

Since then, Rouch's quest has continued, multiform, ramified, accumulating a jumble of ethnological reports, psychodramas, mythologico-burlesque serials, fictions, experiences of every kind and condition which, more or less at the mercy of indefinable circumstances, may become films running twenty minutes or five hours, which may or may not reach the screen, but which are at all events 'films which beget films'—by Rouch and by other film makers.

Translated by Tom Milne